Mexican Ro
A Culinary Journey

Raices Mexicanas

About the authors

Chonette Perez is Mexican and has lived in the United Kingdom since 1970. She is a passionate home cook with many creative interests. She loves gardening, sewing, and the company of close friends and family. In 1986 she established Quetzal, a business dedicated to the promotion of Mexican arts, crafts and culture. She runs Mexican cookery classes and provides consultancy services to businesses, organisations and countless individuals. Her shop, like her restaurant, is an extension of her home, a place where true Mexican hospitality is extended to all.

Anna Xochitl Taylor, Chonette's daughter, is an Art History graduate and teacher. Widely experienced in event and exhibition organising, Anna worked with the National Museums of Scotland before leaving to pursue her passion for all things Mexican. She is Quetzal's Education Officer and teaches in schools, museums and community centres across the United Kingdom. In 2002 she was invited by the Royal Academy of Arts in London to lead workshops for their acclaimed exhibition *Aztecs*. Anna also lectures on Mexican culture. She divides her time between Wiltshire and London.

Both authors have travelled extensively in Mexico. This, their first book, is a record of knowledge and experiences acquired on these journeys.

Mexican Roots

A Culinary Journey Through Time

Discover the delights of real Mexican home cooking

Chonette Perez & Anna Xochitl Taylor

Published by Quetzal Mexican Arts and Crafts

Acknowledgements

We wish to thank all the people we have met on our travels and field trips to Mexico, for they have provided the inspiration for this book. In particular, our deep appreciation to Guadalupe Salinas of Restaurante Nu Luu, in San Felipe del Agua, Oaxaca, for sharing her vast culinary knowledge. Special thanks are due to Maria de Lourdes Rico Arce at the Royal Botanical Gardens Herbarium in London (Kew Gardens) and Louise Schoenhals, for assistance sourcing *nahuatl* names. We are indepted to Jocelyn Timothy and Liz Endrich for their editorial work and support, and to all our Mexican friends in Edinburgh and Wiltshire, especially Claudia Alvarez, Patricia Gallegos, Myrna Reyes, Felicitas Perales and Alejandra Ramirez. We are very grateful to Trevor Lockwood of www.author.co.uk, for his professional advise on all aspects of self publishing, and to Alex Guzman for his valuable technical assistance, support and enduring patience, as what began as a small project soon expanded and took on a life of its own. A heartfelt thank you to everyone who has helped us on this exciting journey.

Cover Photographs and Images:

Front above left: hand-patted *gordas* in Queretaro. **Front above centre:** colonial couryard in Pátzcuaro, Michoacán. **Front above right:** humming bird stamp, found in Yucatán; motif by Jorge Enciso. **Front centre right:** deities (precedessors of the Aztec rain god, Tláloc and Quetzalcoatl, the feathered serpent) on the facade of a pyramid at Teotihuacán, Mexico. **Below left:** poinsettias growing wild in San José Purua, Michoacán. **Back above right:** frying fish and *chiles rellenos* on the shores of Lake Pátzcuaro, Michoacán. **Back centre left:** ceramics on sale in Tzintzuntzán market, Michoacán. **Back below:** fresh fruit and vegetables on sale in the market, Taxco, Guerrero.

First published in Great Britain in 2002 by
Quetzal Mexican Arts and Crafts
61 New Road
Chippenham
Wiltshire
SN15 1ES
www.quetzal-uk.com
info@quetzal-uk.com
Telephone -44-(0)1249-652496

Printed in Great Britain by Anthony Rowe Ltd.
Cover design by Chonette Perez, Anna Taylor and George Penny of Ripe Reprographics Ltd.
Book design by Chonette Perez and Anna Taylor, with technical assistance from Alex Guzman.
Illustrations Alberto Beltran, Heriberto Garcia Rivas and Anna Taylor
Pre-Hispanic design motifs by Jorge Enciso
Photography Chonette Perez and Anna Taylor

Contents

God and goddess of maize, Codex Borgia.

Preface

Food for my spirit

We all have something that keeps us going in life, a lifeboat that keeps us afloat in stormy waters. I have been fortunate, for two lifeboats have accompanied me on my journey through life. The first is my love for gardening and horticulture. Although I have moved frequently, I have created a beautiful garden in every place I have lived. Many regarded me as eccentric for doing so, for they saw little point in it knowing I would be leaving it all behind. But for me, time spent in my garden tending to my plants, has given me strength to cope with any eventuality, however big or small. In 1997 I began a course in Organic Horticulture at The Lackham College of Agriculture, where I discovered that I am not the only person with such a passion.

For many years I was unaware that cooking is my other lifeboat, perhaps because my first attempts at it were so disastrous! During my early working days in Mexico City, when I shared a flat with a close friend Laura, we attempted to cook a *macaroni* dish, a favourite of my aunt's. Although we had followed her instructions diligently, the result was a gooey, sticky mess! Neither of us could understand what we had done, but when it finally occurred to my aunt to ask us if we had remembered to boil the pasta first, we realised where we had gone wrong! Things improved gradually, largely because friends at the office were brave enough to taste my culinary efforts. But by the time I got married, it still took me a whole morning to produce a meal.

During the years that I lived in different parts of the world, I developed an interest in food. I was always fascinated by the local way of cooking. I relished the fresh produce on sale in my local market in Singapore and my years in Germany fuelled my enthusiasm for baking. Many happy hours were spent making biscuits with my children. I always enjoyed hosting dinner parties at home, which gave me the opportunity to try out my cooking and experiment

with menus. I never cooked solely Mexican food for these parties, but always had something on the menu that from Mexico.

Back to my roots

Over the last fifteen years I have gone back to my roots, to cooking the Mexican way. During this time I have come to realise that cooking is the other passion in my life that has kept me afloat. Frequent buying trips to Mexico for my shop 'Quetzal' were a turning point in my interest in Mexican cooking. Seeing how much *Tex-Mex* food was available in the United Kingdom, and hearing how people loved or hated what they imagined was authentic Mexican food, made me want to share with them the taste of *real* Mexican food and how simple it can be to reproduce in the Britain.

Watching the film adaptation of Laura Esquivel's novel 'Like Water for Chocolate' and later reading her book made me see parallels in my own life with cooking. I was not, like Tita, bound to the house and destined to look after my mother until her dying day, but like her, cooking came to be something almost spiritual for me. The preparation of a meal, shared with family and friends, had the potential to turn events and was for me an uplifting experience.

My great uncle emigrated to Mexico from Spain in 1902. My father, and then my sister and I, emigrated shortly after my mother died. My sister and I were brought up by my aunt in Guadalajara in the state of Jalisco, land of eternal spring, home of *mariachi* music, tequila and a place with a fondness for food and celebration. Like most children, we helped out in the kitchen. I was given the task of removing little stones from the beans and lentils before they were thrown in the pot. I have fond memories of trips to local markets and neighbouring villages with my father, who instilled in me a love for Indian Mexico and a pride for a culture that was to become my own.

My father was a simple man at heart and from him I inherited a love for nature and rural life. As a boy he tended goats in his native village of Antoñanzas in La Rioja. Goats pretty much look after themselves, so with much time on his hands he became a voracious reader. "A good education," he always said, "is the best thing you can give your children."

I grew up fast, and had to support myself from an early age. My early working life was spent in advertising, marketing and printing. Working with creative people enhanced my interest in all art forms, the popular arts in particular. I often visited remote villages to study traditional crafts and returned with a car full of purchases. I also helped out a friend who had a stand at the famous *Bazar del Sabado* Saturday market in San Angel, Mexico City.

Entertaining in Mexico

Entertaining in Mexico is a relaxed affair. Friends will come into the kitchen, help prepare the *botanas* and drinks, take dishes away from the table and fetch new ones, without being asked or expected to. It's not up to the host to do every-thing. The evening passes by in a spirit of companionship and every one feels at home and part of the occasion.

Gatherings involving large quantities of delicious food seem to happen so easily in Mexican communities, for on many occasions each person will bring a dish of some kind. In no time at all, a small party is under way. There is no formality or meticulous pre-planning. The gesture is quite spontaneous. This is an atmosphere I have tried to recreate in my own restaurant, which by any standards is far from conventional. For a start, we are not open all the time and most of our bookings are by word of mouth. You have to reserve in advance and your party is welcomed as if into a Mexican home. Sometimes our guests invite us to sit down with them. They even come into the kitchen and offer to help with the washing up! Thankfully I have a dishwasher, so usually we become engrossed in lengthy discussions instead.

My restaurant at 'Quetzal'

Like many things in my life, the restaurant seemed to evolve by itself. Far from starting out as some commercial *concept* or *theme*, it evolved when I began to cook for myself in the shop. The advantage of having a shop is that people can visit you at any time of day and you never know who will walk through the door. Almost inevitably, as if by some twist of fate, they arrive just as you are sitting down to a meal. This is good news in Mexico as there is no such thing as 'cooking for one person'. You always prepare more than you need and adding water to the soup is a common solution to the arrival of unexpected visitors.

Many of our friends, family, customers, artists, travellers, even the occasional salesperson, have ended up sharing food at my table. Soon the suggestions began to creep in, "Why don't you open a coffee shop?" This seemed like a perfect idea. After all, students and those about to embark on travels to Mexico were often consulting our *Education Department* and huge library of books: so why not offer them coffee and cake and make their stay more comfortable? Providing a place where my customers could sit and relax brought with it an unexpected bonus (especially during fraught Christmas shopping sessions). It meant they were more relaxed about those difficult purchase decisions and naturally, sitting down to admire the hand crafted mirrors on the walls and the hand-blown glasses we served from inspired a few more purchases! But I never really ran my business as a *business*. It was more a way of making a living from something I enjoy and promoting a culture that means a lot to me.

In 1998 my daughter Anna arranged for a group of eighteen artists from the Mexican folk dance company *Los Lupeños de San José* to perform at a local festival. This was no mean feat: It all took about a year of organisation. The dancers caused a sensation and 'Mexican Magic' hit the headlines of all the local newspapers. People could not believe there was so much variety of dance and costume in one country, though the performance was just a 'taste' of what awaits discovery in Mexico. I was given the huge task of providing three meals a day for the company. If ever there was a time when my restaurant felt like Mexico, it was during this event. Substantial quantities of food were consumed, the tequila flowed, and the singing and dancing, all highly contagious, continued well into the night.

For all the services we provide, my shop and home have become an unofficial Embassy of Mexico, and even a welfare and counselling service! When you serve someone a cup of tea in a homely setting, they open up to you, and soon they are telling you everything.

Comida Casera
Home cooking

From coffee and cake we gradually progressed to meals. But I wasn't going to make life difficult for myself by planning a complicated menu, nor was I going to provide food already available around the corner. The lunchtime dish was Mexican style *comida corrida* or *comida casera*. On all my many buying and field research trips to Mexico, *comida corrida* has saved the day. This is a set lunch menu, in what is usually a small family run restaurant. Guests are quite happy to order whatever the dish of the day may be. For an incredibly reasonable sum you are served with a soup, either a *sopa aguada* (wet soup), the kind of soup we are accustomed to in the United Kingdom, or *sopa seca*, a dry soup, usually rice or pasta. Then follows a main course dish, which normally consists of meat. Naturally you are never kept waiting without some form of nourishment and often *totopos* (*tortilla* chips), bread or savoury biscuits await you from the moment you take your place at the table. To accompany them, a range of fresh *salsas*, one of which will be *chile* hot. Dessert is a simple affair. If I'm lucky, it's the *flan* or caramel I have a weakness for. Freshly made *aguas* or water drinks, usually lime, orange or *jamaica* are served to quench your thirst.

In this way I began to serve *comida corrida* in my coffee shop, improvising a dish of the day with whatever ingredients were available at the time. This was when I discovered

just how many of my customers were quite happy not to scrutinise a menu and make decisions in a world in which too many decisions must be made as it is. They were content to eat whatever I had cooked, and always came back.

None of the dishes I created were complicated, nor had they absorbed much of my time and concentration, but people often sang praises as if I had produced some gastronomic masterpiece (quite undeserved I felt, as I was simply cooking in the only way I knew how). I came to realise that many of the skills Mexican women utilise everyday were complete unknowns to some of my staff and customers – an understanding of what different ingredients do to a dish, the ability to create delicious food with whatever is at hand, the know-how to run a kitchen like an efficiently run business and the aptitude to plan way ahead so that you too can enjoy the fruits of your labour.

On every trip to Mexico, I made the most of opportunities to learn about food. At many of the craft workshops, where I buy, it is the women who deal with the affairs of business. As a woman I was welcomed almost immediately into the heart of the household: the kitchen. Here preparations were underway for the most meaningful moment in the day, the sharing of food. I had come in pursuit of one art and discovered another, for the dishes they prepared were every bit as skilfully and colourfully created as the hand made pottery pieces, lacquered boxes and woven textiles I had come in search of. I have many fond memories of conversations with waiters, chefs, *taqueros* and market stall vendors, all of whom so readily shared their culinary knowledge with me.

Back in the United Kingdom, focus soon shifted to evening cuisine and dinner parties. Many of the recipes included in this book are those dishes that have been enjoyed by customers in my restaurant. They have motivated and encouraged me to publish this collection of recipes so that they too can have a go at home.

As with so many of my projects, my family have willingly jumped on board. This book is a joint venture.

My daughter Anna and I have edited the recipes together. She has undertaken a study of the cultural significance of food in Mexico and the history of the many products that have come to us from Mexico; maize, tomatoes, courgettes and squash, *chile*, beans, avocados, vanilla and chocolate, to name a few. In recognition of the impact these products have had on world cuisine, and to give credit where it is due, we have arranged the recipes by *product*, rather than the more conventional *Starter, Main Course, Dessert*. We hope that you will explore any section that interests you, in any order.

Anna has always kept journals on her travels around the world. She begins here with an extract she wrote during an eight-month field trip to Mexico, shortly after her eighteenth birthday.

Chonette Perez 2002

Above: detail from a ceramic vase, made in the Suarez family workshop, Tonalá, Jalisco.

Introduction

The Kitchen in the Suarez household

Anna's journal: Tonalá, Jalisco, Mexico. January 1989

The first time I entered Señora Suarez' kitchen in the ceramic producing village of Tonalá, Jalisco, I had the impression, judging by the frenzy of activity, that preparations were underway for an important event, like a family celebration or the visit of a long lost relative. The entire household seemed to be involved. Angelita was busy preparing a hearty breakfast of *huevos rancheros*, eggs 'ranch style'. As she stirred her sauce seductively, an irresistible aroma of sizzling onion, spices and tomato drifted from the stove. With her other hand she skilfully turned *tortillas* on the *comal* or griddle. Martha was ruthlessly shredding the yellow meat of an enormous cooked chicken (I am told that chickens are yellow in Mexico because they are part fed with marigold flowers). Eva was sorting dried beans and Mary was occupied chopping a bunch of freshly picked coriander. Señor Suarez, lethal knife in hand, was slicing sweet, ripe *mamey* fruit for *liquados* or milkshakes. Breakfast and lunch were simultaneously under preparation.

Señora Suarez, a matriarchal figure of domineering character, sat at the large round table overseeing the proceedings, slowly separating *tortillas* into neat piles and wrapping them in cloth to prevent them from drying out. Concerns of the day were under discussion, including a disagreement with a reputable customer. Several times, between *tortillas*, Angelita would turn and voice her strong opinion. My attention shifted to the enormous feast laid out unceremoniously in front of me; large pottery *casuelas* filled with unknown delicacies; a basket of warm freshly made *tortillas*; a huge pot of beans; many different coloured *salsas* (each member of the family had their favourite); *jalapeño chiles*; freshly sliced avocado; watermelon and papaya; shredded lettuce; stringy white cheese and an old paint tub of fresh cream. Suddenly the kitchen door crashed open quite unexpectedly as Luís made an entrance with a large crate of bottled drinks, wiped the sweat from his brow and took his place at the table. Ruben, his elder brother, timed his arrival perfectly, just at the moment when his mother ushered her family to the table.

"*A comer, la mesa esta puesta!'* (Let's eat, food is on the table!).

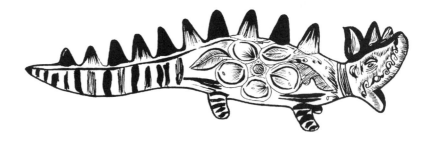

This was in fact a day like any other in the Suarez household, where much time seems to centre on food and its preparation. Appearances are not important: the quality of the food and its flavour mean much more than the presentation. Here the appreciation of fine food is an art form instilled in early childhood. Anyone can taste a dish and tell you exactly what is missing.

It was 11 o'clock in the morning and time for *almuerzo* or brunch. I was awoken at 5.30 a.m. that morning by a horrendous cry from the street of what sounded like a man with a terrible stomach pain. It was in fact the cry of the water seller, *aguaaaa*, whose health, I am told, is in perfect order. The day began early at 6 a.m. for most with a cup of strong coffee and *pan dulce* (sweet bread) before work in the *taller* or ceramic workshop began. Lunch, the main meal of the day, begins any time from 2 to 4 o'clock, comprising of soup, a main course and desert. Sweetbread and coffee or *chocolate* provide early evening nourishment.

As I soon discovered, at different points during the day, when family members emerged clutching yet more delicacies, there is a never ending choice of food available for purchase on the street outside; mangos on sticks, home made crisps, sugared *churros*, freshly steamed hot *tamales*, corn on the cob *con todo* (with everything), everything being lashings of mayonnaise, lime and generous sprinklings of cheese and *chile*. Then there is the ice cream shop and *paleteria* around the corner that sells homemade ice cream and sorbets made with real fruit. Sometimes, during the week when she has time, the lady next-door sells huge slices of her home made cakes from a basket on her doorstep.

Around midnight, just as I was convinced that it was physically impossible to fit another meal into the day, Mary asked if I was coming to try the best *tacos* in the village, if not the whole of Mexico! At Rafa's *taco* stand, the conversation turned to the things I 'must do' before I leave the village and naturally they all centre on food. I must try Señora Cuca's *pozole*, the *carnitas* at *La Flor de Michoacan* and *barbacoa* at the Suarez' *rancho* or ranch. On this day my love affair with Mexican food began!

Travels across Mexico

As anyone who knows me well will tell you, my love for food relates mostly to the pleasure I take in eating it. Mexico is a food lover's paradise, as I was soon to discover, but I had gone there with an altogether different a purpose: I wished to explore the traditional arts and crafts of this vast land. I had developed a passion for Mexican crafts on my first visit to the country as a child. On this trip, a decade later, I was set the seemingly enormous task of building a collection of traditional crafts; two sea containers filled with artefacts for export to the United Kingdom.

As I travelled across Mexico I was overwhelmed by the flare and creativity of the Mexican people. From the colourful threads of a hand embroidered *huipil* or blouse to a simple arrangement of fruit in the market place, art and colour permeate every aspect of life in Mexico. Objects for everyday use are often beautifully decorated; simple clay pots and dishes for cooking, carved wooden spoons, lacquered gourds for gathering grain and liquids, even the most humble of objects is embellished by the hand of an artist. In Mexico there is no dividing line between art and everyday life. The same pot that earns the praise of a collector is put to use in the Mexican home. Many of the artefacts I encountered played a part in the preparation and serving of food and drink.

It soon became clear to me that Mexico is a country where food means so much more than nourishing the body. At every event I attended, food was the single most important consideration, whether a wedding, a baptism, a birthday or a simple gathering of friends and family. Year round, a wealth of celebrations crowd the Mexican calendar; Independence Day, *Dia de la Raza*, the Day of the Dead, Revolution Day, the Feast of Guadalupe, Christmas, Epiphany, *Dia de la Candelaria*, carnival, Easter and *Cinco de Mayo* among many. Food is an essential part of all these festivities.

To take part in the preparation of real Mexican food is to experience living history. In many indigenous communities in particular, food has religious significance and is often associated with ancient ritual and beliefs. Great things happen around the dinner table; the spirits of the harvest are honoured, family relationships are fostered, friendships are bonded, revolutions planned and the souls of the dead are reunited with the living.

A trip to market in Mexico, to purchase fresh produce, is a pleasurable, tactile experience. Hand patting a maize *tortilla*, wrapping a *tamal* and toasting peppers on the *comal* are every bit as prestigious an art as painting a fine ceramic vessel. Adela Fernandez, daughter of the film director Emilio Fernandez, speaks of the early years of her life, bound by service to the home. Far from viewing this as a burden, she makes the following revelation in the foreword of her book *Traditional Mexican Cooking:*

"I am more than aware that it was those times spent in the kitchen that awakened me to the history of my people, that helped me understand our cultural heritage, turned me into an artist and made me love Mexico more dearly. The kitchen was the very nerve centre of our house, a vast melting pot of ideals."

My own role in my mother's restaurant began as chief taster, but soon I had to learn to cook. When she was away on business and we had important bookings, I was handed the wooden spoon and the *tortilla press*. I was not too pleased about this at first: I was no cook, but let this be encouragement to you! However, when I discovered that cooking is a creative process as opposed to a chore, it brought me closer to my roots. If I inherit nothing else, I consider this a worthwhile legacy.

Helping in the restaurant also brought about positive changes in my life. I am no longer fazed at the prospect of inviting 50 people to dinner and seeing the real pleasure people take in the whole dinning experience is very fulfilling. I now find that I can produce a simple meal without much effort. Unless you really enjoy what you do, I am a great believer in economy of effort. If, like me, you are a busy person, or if fussing in the kitchen is not your thing, you could learn a lot from a nation of people who are masters at improvisation and at producing a delicious meal with whatever is at hand.

Cooking in the modern world

It is hardly surprising that nowadays many people do not make time for cooking. Unless we are farmers, many of us have become totally detached from the process of producing and preparing food. We are so used to finding everything we need and crave for in the supermarket that we rarely stop to think where food has come from and how different things were as recently as fifty years ago. Many are unaware that our food has a long and fascinating history.

As a teacher, I have taught many children who actually believe that milk comes from the supermarket! For them, going to market and handpicking vegetables in season is a thing of the past. But they can tell me all about the *beep* a barcode makes at the checkout and how many tokens they have collected from their favourite cereal packet! Because they are eager to learn about the products that interest them, they are fascinated when I tell them that the Aztecs invented popcorn, and that they used cocoa beans as currency. Few children in the United Kingdom have seen cocoa pods and beans. One little girl thought they were dog biscuits! Now that they know all about chocolate, these children tell me they appreciate it all the more. We hope that by learning more about all the ingredients included in this book, you too will come to appreciate them.

What and how we eat tells us a great deal about ourselves, about the priorities in our lives, our hopes and aspirations, our feelings towards friends and family, the importance of tradition in our lives and our concern or lack of concern for our health. Whatever we feel about our food, most of us are or may one day be responsible for placing a meal on the table. It is an inspiration to us all to learn from a culture that has made the every day pursuit of cooking a meal so utterly meaningful.

Misconceptions about Mexican food

Many myths exist about Mexican food, largely because most of the 'Mexican food' available in the United Kingdom is not the real thing. Tex-Mex is more common than *true-Mex*. Mexico is an enormous country (about eight times the size of Great Britain). Every region has its own style of cooking. With so much variety from region to region and even from village to village, there are dishes to suit every conceivable taste and dietary requirement. If *Mexican food* sounds exotic or alien, consider the fact that many of the foods we take for granted today (maize, tomatoes, beans, *chiles*, avocadoes, courgettes, chocolate and vanilla) were once strange and exotic to our ancestors. All have come to us from Mexico and the lands that once belonged to her.

One of my mother's reasons for writing this book is to dispel the popular myth that all Mexican food is hot and spicy. *Chile* is added to many dishes in Mexico for flavour, but not all dishes are hot. It often comes as a surprise to her customers when she tells them that not all Mexican people like hot, spicy food. Some of her customers worry about bringing along *fussy* friends, but their fears are usually unfounded.

How to use this book

Recipes and techniques

This is a book you can read your way through or cook your way through. The recipes are arranged according to product (maize, *chile*, bean…), but you can dip into them in any order. If you are interested in *botanas* or appetizers, for example, you will find them under *Maize, Chilli, Bean, Marrow, Tomato* and *Avocado*. There are *salsas* under *Tomato, Chilli* and *Avocado*. Similarly, soups are found under most of the savoury sections. If it is basic techniques you are after, for example, *How to handle chiles* or *How to make tomato sauce,* you will find them in the appropriate section. Basic methods for preparing rice and chicken are listed under *Mole and Pumpkin Seed Sauces,* the sauces they often accompany. These techniques can be combined with or applied to cooking from any country.

Most of the recipes are suitable for vegetarians because Mexicans naturally use vegetables, seeds and pulses in their cooking. If you have special dietary requirements, you have a great deal of choice. Mexican food is dependent on maize, providing a perfect gluten-free diet. Try the fruit caramels for desserts without dairy products.

Do not be put off by the length of some of the recipes. They are not as complicated as they may appear. Making *tortillas*, for example, takes time, but is well worth the effort. Because my mother has experience running cookery courses, she knows the problems you are likely to encounter. She includes in her recipes everything she would tell you if she were with you in person. She is a practical person, who thrives on contact with people. If you have any queries or feedback, you are welcome to get in touch through our website.

With the exception of one or two, most of the recipes in this book have been prepared with ingredients readily available in the United Kingdom. Where appropriate, suitable substitutes are suggested (Wensleydale cheese, for example, crumbles like *queso fresco*). The emphasis is on the underlying principals for preparing authentic Mexican food.

You can be creative and apply these to your own cooking. The approach is practical and modern because we would much rather the dishes were prepared. The key is to use fresh ingredients and freeze the sauces and soups if you can. That way you can produce a delicious meal in no time when you need to. By adding a few fresh ingredients, a sauce will taste the same as the day you made it.

We have written this book for anyone who appreciates good food. Whether your interest is eating, cooking or entertaining, we hope you will be inspired to have a go at the recipes. *Mexican Roots* reflects our love for history, cookery, horticulture and travel. Whatever your passion in life, we invite you will join us on this culinary journey.

Buen apetito y buen provecho!

The Great Aztec Market of Tlatelolco.

The Market

The Great Aztec Market of Tlatelolco

"We were astounded at the great number of people and the quantities of merchandise, and at the orderliness and good arrangements that prevailed, for we had never seen such a thing before."
"Some of our soldiers who had been in many parts of the world, in Constantinople, in Rome, and all over Italy, said that they had never seen a market so well laid out, so large, so orderly, and so full of people." Bernal Díaz del Castillo

Bernal Díaz del Castillo, who served under Cortés wrote his chronicle "The Conquest of New Spain" some fifty years after the Conquest of Mexico. When he and the other Spanish conquistadors reached the mighty Aztec capital of Tenochtitlan in 1519, the sight of the great *tianguis* or open market of Tlatelolco clearly overwhelmed them.

Díaz del Castillo describes the enormous variety of goods on display. *"If I describe everything in detail I shall never be done,"* he says. He mentions first the dealers in gold, silver, precious stones, feathers, cloaks and embroidered goods. He describes cotton and fabric merchants and those who sold a variety of animal skins such as jaguar and deerskins. There were sellers of timber, tobacco, paper and reeds. In another part of the market pottery of all kinds was sold.

There were sellers of beans and vegetables in one place and herbs in another. There were merchants, who sold fowl, turkey, birds, rabbits, deer, ducks and little dogs. There were also fruit sellers and women who sold all kinds of cooked food, flour and honey. Every product had its own particular section in the market and trade was overseen by supervisors and judges who settled disputes. The majority of goods were bartered or exchanged. Cocoa beans, feathers and gold were used as currency.

The Museum of Anthropology in Mexico houses a wonderful detailed model of the Tlatelolco market. Another magnificent representation is the mural of Aztec life in the Palacio Nacional, painted by the great Mexican muralist

Diego Rivera. Here in the heart of Mexico City, centre of the former Aztec capital, the observer is invited to gaze in awe at the marvels of the ancient world.

In Aztec times, goods were transported across the Empire by merchants called *pochteca*. Illustration from Sahagún's Codex Florentino.

The Mexican Market Today

The market in Mexico today stems from an ancient tradition. Visit some of Mexico's largest permanent markets, such as *La Merced, Sonora* and *Jamaica* markets in Mexico City, and *San Juan de Dios* in Guadalajara, and you sense that this tradition is still very much alive. The sense of order still prevails. Areas are divided according to produce; fresh fruit and vegetables in one, dried herbs and *chiles* in another, meat and fish in another. Getting lost in one of these markets is a day out in itself. Amidst the hustle and bustle, a resting-place is always close at hand. Some of the best food is sold in the market place along with fresh fruit *liquados* or milk shakes and freshly squeezed fruit juices.

Markets in Mexico are a kaleidoscope of colour, teaming with life and activity. Though most cities and towns have covered permanent markets nowadays, the tradition of the market or *tianguis* day lives on, from the *barrio* of the City to the remotest rural village. Even in cities, where a supermarket may be just round the corner, people prefer to select fresh fruit and vegetables at the weekly market. Knowing how to select the finest produce is an acquired skill and art. Shopping becomes a highly tactile experience. Fruits and vegetables, beans, maize, spices, sweets, pots and pans, domestic wares, toys, ornaments, handicrafts…in fact almost anything, depending on the region, can be found in the Mexican marketplace. The market is a highly sociable place;

people come as much to buy and sell as to exchange news and enjoy the atmosphere.

In rural areas people travel far to market day to sell their home grown produce and wares. Here the market is the pulse of the local community. Where there is business there is great initiative and sound commercial sense. Bartering is a natural part of the buying-selling experience, an acquired skill that requires intelligence, good humour and a friendly spirit.

Market scene from a ceramic plate, made in Tzintzuntzán, Michoacán. Popular arts frequently mirror scenes from everyday life.

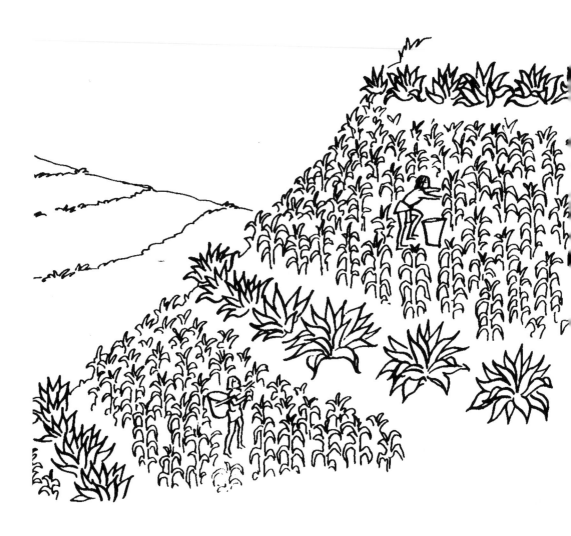

The Aztecs practiced terraced cultivation in the moutainous areas of Central Mexico, turning the contours of the land into productive farming terrain. Maguey plants, grown close together, formed walls that prevented soil errosion.

Pre-Hispanic Roots

Colossal statue of a woman, believed to be the water goddess Chalchiutlicue, *Lady of the Jade Skirt*. Discovered near the pyramid of the Moon, Teotihuacán. 350-650 AD 3.9m, 22 tons. Museum of Anthropology, Mexico City.

Mexico is a land of geographical diversity; home to vast deserts, tropical rainforests, snow-capped mountains and fertile valleys. Together they sustain one of the most varied collections of plant and animal species in the world. By the time of the Spanish Conquest, in the sixteenth century, the ancient Mexicans were the greatest plant cultivators in the world. They developed a sophisticated understanding of the natural world. Over many centuries, thousands of wild plants were exploited for medicinal and practical purposes. Others were domesticated to form crops then unknown outside the Americas; maize, amaranth, pumpkin, bean, *chile*, tomato, avocado, vanilla and cocoa among them. The cultivation of maize, the most important of all these crops, gave rise to the great civilisations of ancient Mexico; the Huastec, the Zapotec, the Mixtec, the Maya, the Tarascans, the Toltec and the Aztec.

Divine Intervention

Agriculture held a spiritual dimension in pre-Hispanic Mexico. The rainfall pattern was fundamental, so the cult of gods of water and vegetation absorbed much of religious life. The most important of these gods was Tláloc, god of rain, who the Maya called Chac. For the Mixtec it was Tzahui and the Zapotec, Cocijo. A giant statue found in Teotihuacán, believed to be the water goddess Chalchiuhtlicue, is one of the largest worked stone blocks in Mesoamerica. The Aztecs also venerated Chicomecóatl, goddess of sustenance, and in addition each important crop had its own divine character. According to Aztec legend, *Tlalocan* (paradise) was the abode of Tláloc, the god of rain, a place where maize, pumpkin, *chile*, tomatoes and beans grew in abundance.

The giant Aztec rain god Tláloc once resided in the community of Coatlinchán. Today he stands at the entrance of the Museum of Anthropology in Mexico City c.900 AD.

Agriculture continues to be the principal occupation of indigenous populations today. Although most Mexicans are catholic, many pre-Hispanic beliefs persist. In the Texcoco area, near the pyramids of Teotihuacán, shamen or *graniceros* (rain makers) still communicate with the spiritual domains of Tláloc. Journalist Maria Rivera describes the work of a respected rainmaker, Timoteo Hernandez, in her article "A Torrential Downpour will cost you 1500 pesos". Timoteo, or Don Timo, as he is known locally, is from the village of Tequesquinahuac on the slopes of mount Tláloc. He explains that he cannot guarantee precision when he petitions the rain; sometimes it will rain a few days before, sometimes a few days after. At times the rain falls exactly were he intends, but on other occasions the entire village may be deluged. But there will always be rain.

In Tequesquinahuac, the festival of Santa Cruz is celebrated each year in May. Although this festival is Christian, the date corresponds with a pre-Hispanic festival, *Huey tozoztli*, once dedicated to Tláloc. Local people decorate sacred crosses with flowers and make offerings of food to the spirits; *tortillas*, beans, rice, *mole*, fruit, sweets, even beer and coffee are offered. At the close of the festival Don Timo makes an appeal for rain, to protect the harvest.

Whereas his ancestors venerated idols, Don Timo adorns an altar with an image of 'The Virgin of the Lightening Ray', who is surrounded by images of Christ, the Virgin of Guadalupe and other Christian saints. Don Timo's eighty-four year old father Don Tacho, also a rainmaker, speaks of a time when the great monolithic statue of Tláloc, adored by his ancestors, resided in the community of San Miguel Coatlinchán. His words are evidence of a fusion of ancient and Christian beliefs. "They say it is bad to worship this stone," says Don Tacho, "but I believe that God has blessed him and given him spirit." Don Tacho believes the spirit of the stone is still alive and that it has a soul. How else can you explain the fact that it has been raining in Mexico City ever since the statue was taken there, he asks? He has a point. My mother remembers, as if it were yesterday, the day the 168 tonne statue of Tláloc was ceremoniously transported to Mexico City, despite local protest. Like Don Tacho, locals believed the pattern of rainfall would be affected forever. They may be right. Four decades ago rain was abundant, but now, largely due to deforestation and global climate change, rainfall is scarce. This means more work for rainmakers like Don Timo, who make contact with supernatural forces.

Some people called it coincidence, but on the day that Tláloc was transported to Mexico City, it rained heavily all through the night, though it was not the rain season. Even the non-superstitious began to wonder when it poured with rain every time the great statue was moved! The domain of Tláloc, one of the oldest gods of Mesoamerica, is still very much alive. Today he guards the entrance to the Museum of Anthropology in Mexico City, one of the finest museums in the world.

An Abundance of Crops

The people of ancient Mexico were essentially vegetarians. Farming methods varied according to the region. The Aztec capital Tenochtitlán (*Place of the Prickly-Pear Cactus*), was built on land reclaimed from a great lake. The Aztecs employed a sophisticated method of growing crops on

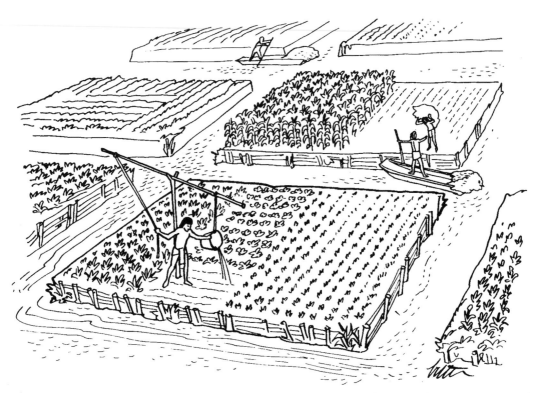

Aztec chinampa gardens supplied the capital with a rich variety of fresh crops.

chimampas, fertile plots built with layers of vegetation and thick mud from the bottom of the lake. This mud, produced from volcanic ashes, was rich in minerals. The *chinampas* provided an ingenious method of self-irrigation, one that is still practised in Xochimilco today; the plots were built high so the roots of the crops were not rotted by the lake, but low enough to absorb moisture. A Cyprus tree called *Abuehuete* (Taxodium mucronatum) was planted around the edge of the *chinampas* to stabilize the plots.

In outlying areas, fields were built with a series of canals for irrigation and fertilized with silt and manure. In hilly areas, plots were terraced. The land was worked by hand with strong hard wood digging sticks. Organic farming was practised; a variety of crops and flowers were planted together, such as maize, beans, *chile* and marigold.

The pre-Hispanic diet, which combined maize, pumpkin, *chile* and bean, was highly nutritious. Other vegetables cultivated or collected from the wild, included tomatoes, avocados, nopal cactus, maguey, chayote, camote (sweet potato), yucca, jícama (a root vegetable), various root plants and *xonácatl* (a type of onion).

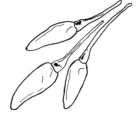

Other grains, seeds and nuts consumed included amaranth, *chia*, peanuts, pine nuts, pumpkin and sunflower seeds. Fruits included *tunas* (prickly pear), *zapote*, *zarzamora* (a type of blackberry), mamey, papaya, *guanábana*, guava, *tejocote* and pineapple.

Culinary Delicacies

Meat did not contribute significantly to the average pre-Hispanic diet. The only animals domesticated for food were dogs, turkeys and ducks. Deer and peccary (wild pig) were hunted and smaller animals such as rabbits were caught in nets. Other birds and animals included pheasant, quail, heron, squirrel, armadillo, iguana, lizard, snake and tortoise. A variety of fresh and saltwater fish were consumed, together with seafood and other aquatic creatures like frogs.

The Spanish chronicler Bernal Díaz del Castillo describes the magnificent daily feast of the Aztec emperor Moctezuma. " *They cooked more than three hundred plates of food the great Montezuma was going to eat, and more than a thousand for the guard.*" The Spanish were amazed at the variety of dishes on offer, too numerous to mention in detail. Among them Díaz describes cooked fowl, turkeys, pheasants, local partridge, quail, duck, venison, boar, marsh birds, pigeons, hares and rabbits. The emperor chose only a fraction, and when he was done, the guards and servants ate in their turn.

Ordinary people supplemented their diet with insect

Pottery iguana from the village of Amatenango, Chiapas.

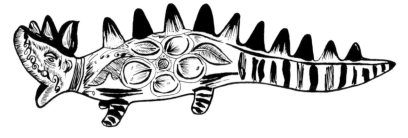

delicacies such as grasshoppers, maguey larva, ants and *jumil* bugs, which were high in protein. I have tried fried *jumiles* made into *salsa*, and they are really tasty. When I sampled a *taco de gusano* (a maguey worm *taco*) I thought it was delicious, until I was told what it was. I believe our aversion to these things is largely cultural.

I was once given a *torta* (crusty roll) with live insects in a Oaxaca market and told to eat it quick before it walked off! I declined at the time as I drew the line at eating anything alive. Also relished by the Aztecs was an alga, high in protein, known as *tecuitlatl* (Spirulina geitlerii), gathered from the surface of the lake.

Sweetness came largely in the form of bee's honey and from maize, maguey and fruit syrup. Cocoa, cultivated in tropical regions and consumed in the form of a bitter beverage, was sweetened with honey and vanilla.

Pre-Hispanic methods of cooking and preserving food

Two basic methods were used to cook food in pre-Hispanic Mexico: grilling and boiling. Food was grilled or toasted on the *comal* or griddle to diffuse the heat, or cooked directly on the flame or ashes. Food was also cooked in holes in the ground, as *barbacoa* is today. The other basic method employed was boiling or steaming (as *tamales* are cooked today). Frying was a Spanish concept, introduced after the Conquest, when animal fat was more widely available. To preserve their food, the people of ancient Mexico dried or salted fish and meat. Grains, *chiles* and seeds were also dried. Maize was stored in a special corn bin called the *cuezcomate*, which is still in use in rural areas today.

Tools

A variety of tools and utensils were used in pre-Hispanic times for the preparation, cooking, serving and storage of food, most of which are still in use today. Mexicans maintain that the taste is just not the same if you cook in modern saucepans. *Guacamole* and *salsas* have a better flavour if they

are pounded in a *molcajete* and beans will take on the earthy taste of the clay pot they are cooked in.

El metate ...*grind the corn*

The *metate*, still in use in rural Mexico today, was the most important utensil in the pre-Hispanic home. Made of porous volcanic stone, the *metate* is a flat rectangular stone that curves up slightly at the ends. It is raised slightly on stone feet and slopes outwards so that the *molendera* or maize grinder can kneel comfortably behind it. The *metlapil* or arm, which is made of the same stone, is used to grind and mash cooked maize into dough. The *metate* is also used to grind *chiles* and other grains, the irregularity of the surface assisting in the grinding process.

The story of my *metate*

As container loading day drew near on my first major buying trip to Mexico, I thought of all the things I had ever wanted to send home that were far too big or heavy to transport by air. A *metate* was one thing that sprang to mind. On market day I seized the opportunity and carried one back to the warehouse, applauded by many street vendors on my way. When the container arrived at the port in England, customs officials were puzzled about an item of 'volcanic rock'. I hadn't imagined the trouble it would cause! The container was delayed as customs officials pondered over what they thought might be an enormous piece of industrial granite, or some kind or meteorite. Why was I bringing it over if it had 'no commercial value'? Was I some kind of fossil enthusiast? You can imagine their reaction when my mother explained that the item was simply a kitchen tool. My humble *metate* has since appeared in countless exhibitions and as part of my handling collection has been tested by hundreds of British school children. I now feel reassured that it was all worthwhile!

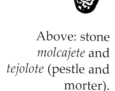

Volcanic stone *metate*, used for grinding maize.

El molcajete...*pound the chiles...*

Second in importance to the *metate*, the *molcajete* is a mortar, and the *tejolote* is the pestle. Made from the same dark volcanic rock as the *metate*, the *molcajete* is used to pound ingredients such as tomatoes, *chile* and spices. In pre-Hispanic times, *molacajetes* were also made of clay. People in Michoacán, with its volcanic landscape, have told us that their *molcajetes* are the best. When you buy a new one in the market, it has to be cured before it is used for the first time (to remove lose stone particles). The *molcajete* becomes seasoned with use, which improves the flavour of the food.

Above: stone *molcajete* and *tejolote* (pestle and morter).

Right: ancient ceramic *molcaje*.

El comal...*cook the tortillas...*

The *comal* or *comalli*, as it was known, is a baked clay disk or griddle, used to cook *tortillas* and other foods. The comal is about fifty centimetres in diameter and is usually placed on three stones, high enough to be heated, without coming into contact with the flames. Today most *comales* are made of metal and modern kitchens have them built into the cooker.

El comal le digo a la olla…

A famous song by the Mexican children's lyricist Gavilondo Soler or *Cri Cri el grillito cantor* (the singing grasshopper), is a playful exchange between the *comal* and the *olla* (the griddle and the cooking pot)

El comal le dijo a la olla
Oye olla, oye, oye
Si te has creido que yo soy recargadera
Buscate otro, que te apoye

Comal or griddle.

Part of the humour is derived from the rhythm of the Spanish words *oye*, *olla* and *apoye*, but as always the ingenuity is lost entirely in the translation!

The griddle said to the cooking pot,
Listen cooking pot, listen, listen,
If you think I'm just something to lean on,
Look for another to support you.

El comitalli

…steam the tamales…

The *comitalli* was a kind of ancient pressure cooker or steamer, a clay pot filled with a little water. A rack was inserted and *tamales*, cooked by the steam, were inserted on top.

Ancient pots and dishes

…cook the beans…

An infinite number of pots, dishes, colanders, plates, cups and jugs were shaped by hand from clay. The potter's wheel and glazing was introduced by the Spanish. However, many ancient methods are still practised today, in villages such as San Bartolo Coyotepec in Oaxaca and Amatenango del Valle in Chiapas.

Classic Maya ceramic bowl, depicts a woman working maize dough on a *metate*.

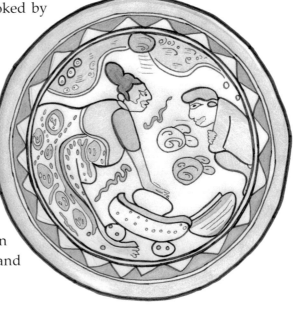

Baskets, gourds and kitchen utensils

Baskets made of different vegetable fibres were used to store and transport food. Gourds were used to store and serve liquids and food. Knives were made of stone or obsidian, some as sharp as a surgeon's knife, and other utensils were made of wood.

Hand made ceramic pot, Amatenango, Chiapas.

The Great Exchange

The Spanish were lured to the Americas by the prospect of gold, but for the Aztecs, gold was a dead, inert metal. Far more precious was jade, symbol of water and life. Although the Spanish did not know it at the time, the plants and animals they took back to Europe were worth infinitely more than their weight in gold; maize, tomatoes, beans, *chiles*, avocados, sweet potatoes, pineapples, vanilla, cocoa, sunflowers, dahlias, poinsettias, peanuts, cotton, turkeys, red cochineal dye, rubber...all were introduced to Europe. Together they constitute Mexico's great gift to humanity. World cuisine was transformed forever and maize, together with potato from South America, ensured human survival. *The Great Exchange*, as it is often called, was one of the most significant outcomes of the Conquest.

The Spanish brought oats, rye and wheat to Mexico, the principle grain of Europe, and with them the tradition of bread making. The Spaniards were great meat eaters and introduced cows, sheep, chickens and pigs to Mexico. Pigs in particular were adaptable and popular. Soon other Old World delicacies arrived; rice, carrots, onion, garlic, coriander, almonds, olive oil, citrus fruits, apples, peaches and pears. Horses, donkeys and oxen were shipped over and immediately set to work. Sugar cane was introduced to the Caribbean, but at a grim cost. Millions of slaves were forcibly transported from Africa to work the plantations.

Epidemics of European diseases, which local people had no resistance to, wiped out vast proportions of the native population across the Americas. In Mexico the population was reduced from about 25 million in 1519, to fewer than

2 million in 1580. Without the 1521 smallpox epidemic, Cortés and his men may never have succeeded in their Conquest.

The Impact of the Spanish Conquest

The sixteenth century encounter between the Spanish and native American peoples was a collision of cultures, an extraordinary event that changed the course of world history and civilisation. It is hard to appreciate this from a twenty-first century viewpoint, but the experience may have been akin to explorers of our own age coming into contact with extraterrestrial life. Ancient Mexico was changed forever. As a result of their physical conquest the Spanish initiated a radical 'spiritual conquest' to convert the native people to Catholicism. Temples, statues and precious painted books, branded as pagan idolatry, were destroyed forever. Despite this, almost five hundred years later, over sixty indigenous groups still preside in Mexico; they speak their own languages and have preserved ancient customs, rituals and traditions.

Below: sunflower design from a ceramic plate, Dolores Hidalgo, Guanjuato. Sunflowers, poinsettias and dahlias were introduced to Europe from Mexico. The Spanish brought roses to Mexico.

The Spanish rejected many of the native Mexican culinary practises as they hindered the spiritual cause. The cultivation of amaranth, for example, or *hautli* as the Aztecs called it, was prohibited because of its religious and ritual significance. Had it not been, amaranth, largely a forgotten grain, would probably play a greater role in world cuisine today. During an Aztec ceremony known as *teoqualo*, an image of Huitzilopochtli, the war god, was created in human form.

The figure was symbolically sacrificed, cut and distributed for consumption amongst festival participants. The Spanish did their best to eradicate this custom because it clashed with the ideology of the Christian communion. They considered it offensive and even went to the extreme of proclaiming amaranth an evil crop.

Today amaranth is used to make sweets called *allegrias*, the word *allegria* meaning joy or happiness. Figures are still made with amaranth, sometimes in the form of national heroes like Benito Juarez. At the time of the *Day of the Dead* celebrations, amaranth seeds are made in the form of cheerful looking skulls, decorated with nuts and colourful chocolate drops. They are sold in markets alongside toys and decorated sugar skulls. This festival is a fusion of pre-Hispanic and European beliefs. It is a happy time when souls of the departed are remembered and return to share food with the living.

Other culinary practises, which the Spanish resisted, were the consumption of insects, algae and dogs. Dogs are no longer eaten in Mexico. The cultural clash was not only restricted to the choice of ingredients, but also to different perceptions of food. The Spaniards did not just eat to satisfy hunger, they ate and drank in excess for the shear pleasure of it. Their habits were gluttonous compared with the more frugal style of the indigenous people. In Aztec society drunkenness was frowned upon. Drinking was only permitted at certain religious ceremonies, and only the elderly could drink freely.

Initially, the first Spaniards in Mexico were served by indigenous cooks and so became accustomed to the native ingredients and style of cooking. The first evangelists to arrive in Mexico were the monks of the Franciscan, Agustin and Dominican orders. They set about compiling detailed records of thousands of indigenous plants and medicines, vast knowledge that had been acquired in ancient Mexico over many centuries. Although credit is rarely given where it is due, Western pharmacology and horticulture was greatly enriched as a result. It is said that the conquistadors preferred Aztec healers to Spanish surgeons, who at times left them worse off!

Theatrical plays, incorporating elements of European history, politics and religion were enacted to further the Christian mission, often followed by grand feasts. Although the diet of the friars was frugal at first, it became excessive in later years once primary objectives had been fulfilled.

In the case of the female religious orders, which arrived later, things were different. Their diet was sparing and marked by periods of fasting and abstinence, except on feast days when lavish banquets were prepared in honour of the visiting Viceroys and archbishops. Old World delicacies, such as sweets, were prepared with New World ingredients. Drawing on the legacy of native culinary techniques, the nuns created dishes, which today are considered amongst the most representative of Mexican cuisine, such as *Chiles en Nogada* and *Mole Poblano*. The daughters of families of mixed marriages (Spanish and indigenous) were often educated in the convents and so these recipes were past on to them.

As European cooks used native ingredients to cook their way, so the indigenous people cooked with European products in the way familiar to them. A true *mestizaje* or marriage of cultures took place. Spanish cuisine is itself *mestizo*, a marriage of Roman, Greek and Arab influences (garlic from Egypt, olives from Greece and citrus and sugar cane from Persia).

International Influences

Every nationality that settled in Mexico integrated with the local community, thus enclaves of exclusively foreign communities are less common than in other parts of the world. All nationalities have married into Mexican families, who are welcoming and highly hospitable. Mexican cuisine

today is therefore a fusion of many different influences, not only Spanish and indigenous.

France made a decisive impact during the French occupation of Mexico in the nineteenth century. The enormous variety of French breads and pastries found in Mexico today, the wide use of savoury crêpes, the popularity of *crema fresca* (creme fraîche) and the national passion for crème caramel desserts affirm this. The famous *tacos al pastor*, cooked on a rotisserie, bear the mark of the Lebanese community; the Italians introduced ice-cream and a preference for pasta and cheese and the Germans brought beer making. The British have also contributed; when the tin mining industry collapsed in Cornwall, Cornish engineers travelled to Mexico to work in local mines and took Cornish pasties with them. Custard in Mexico is known as *crema inglesa* (English cream), roast beef is served with *salsa gravy* (gravy) and *salsa inglesa* is Worcester sauce, used widely in Mexico for cooking. Thoroughly *Mexicanised* American fast food and diner outlets appear in all major cities and resorts, alongside cuisines from all over the world.

In response to international trends, traditional Mexican cuisine has been reinterpreted in recent years to form beautifully presented *nouvelle cuisine*. This *new* or *high* Mexican cuisine is known as *Nueva* or *Alta Cocina Mexicana*. Thoroughly modern and refined, this culinary art preserves and revives important elements of Mexico's past. Despite myriad global influences, the roots of Mexican cooking today remain firmly embedded in Mexico's pre-Hispanic past. There are many things in modern Mexico that past inhabitants would recognise: food is one of them. Maize, particularly in the form of *tortillas*, is consumed by all sectors of Mexican society today, as it has been for centuries. As dusk approaches, vendors of *tamales* (steamed *masa*) and *atole* (porridge) set up stall in towns and villages across Mexico. People from all walks of life gather to relish these delicacies, just as they did in ancient times.

Talavera ceramic plate from Puebla, Mexico. This style and technique of ceramic was introduced to Spain from Morocco, and to Mexico after the Spanish Conquest in the sixteenth century.

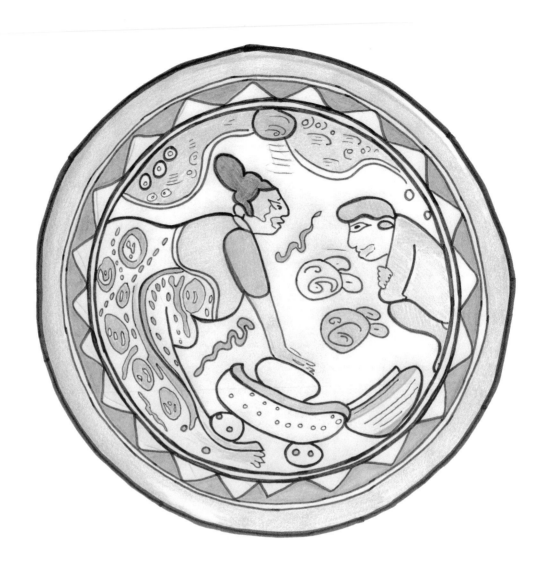

Illustration of a classic Maya bowl, showing a woman working maize
dough on a stone *metate*.

Maize

El maiz - Tlaoli - Zea mays

The Sacred Crop

Maize or corn is without doubt the greatest gift that Mexico has given the world. Alongside wheat and rice, maize is one of the three basic cereal crops that sustains humanity. Today millions of people throughout the world depend on maize for their survival. Highly productive and nutritious, this cereal is extremely adaptable and can be grown in many different environments and climates. One ear of modern corn produces about one thousand large kernels. Writer-historian Karl Meyer estimates that in about four months, without irrigation, a family of three can grow twice as much maize as they can consume in a year. This is a remarkable rate of productivity.

The story of maize cultivation is made more extraordinary by one fact: maize cannot reseed itself without human intervention, for its husks prevent seed dispersal. We have the inhabitants of ancient Mexico to thank for the gift of corn. Over thousands of years and through great skill and patience, they succeeded in domesticating maize from a wild grass called *teosintli* or *teosinte*. No other cultivated plant has undergone such dramatic change. Tiny corn cobs found in caves in Mexico's Tehuacán Valley may date back to 5000 BC. The discovery that *teosinte* might be edible and genetically pliable had phenomenal implications: the results in the Americas were a shift from nomadic hunting to agriculture and settled life.

The great civilisations of Mesoamerica evolved and flourished because of maize. Without the daily concern of food provision, they were free to develop culture and the arts; to build great cities, mighty pyramids and study the wonders of the cosmos. They were liberated by maize.

Grateful for the gift of corn, the ancient Mexicans held the plant as sacred. Maize was central to their myths of

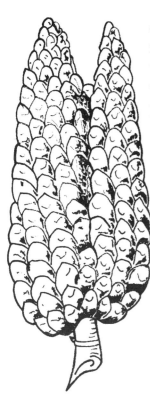

Below: double maize cob, Codex Florentino. The concept of duality, typified by images of life and death in unison, was a recurrent theme in pre-Hispanic art.

God and goddess of maize, Codex Borgia.

creation and to religious life. For the Maya, maize provided nourishment for both body and spirit. According to the Maya legend, the *Popul Vuh*, man was created from maize. The gods had first tried to mould the human form from clay, but it folded under its own weight. They used wood, but this lacked wisdom and had no soul. And so they made dough from maize to form the body of man. Maize became his blood and gave him life and great strength.

For the Aztecs too, maize became legend. An ancient myth tells how the god Quetzalcoatl descended into the kingdom of Mictlantecuhtli, god of death. Here he gathered up the bones of men and women who had lived there before, and with the help of Coatlicue, the goddess of fertility, ground up the bones with his blood to form dough. This he moulded into the human shape of new man.

Quetzalcoatl was puzzled over what this new being should live from, until he saw a tiny ant carrying a kernel of corn. When the ant refused to tell him where the corn had come from, Quetzalcoatl changed himself into a black ant and followed him to Tonacatepetl (the Mound of the Cornfields) where the corn was stored. Quetzalcoatl took back to the gods the corn they fed to humankind. One nahuatl or Aztec word for corn, *tzintli*, was derived from the huastec word *iziz centli* meaning *grain of an ant*.

Maize featured prominently in Aztec religion. There were many gods associated with maize, the principal bring Centeotl (Tzinteotl). There were gods associated with the different stages of corn's development and parts of the plant itself: Centeoticihuatl was the god of ripe maize; Xilonen was the goddess of tender corn; Xipe-totec was god of maize cultivation and Chicomecóatl (7 snakes or 7 corn cobs) goddess of sustenance. Holding a staff, which symbolized fertility, Chicomecóatl was guardian of this most cherished crop. The Franciscan friar Bernardino de Sahagún describes how Aztec women kept cobs of corn from the previous years harvest and hung them before Chicomecóatl. They made an image of the goddess out of dough and offered every kind of maize and vegetable to her.

Rituals surrounding the growth of maize were carried out throughout the year in honour of its deities; villagers cut fine young stalks of maize and decked them with flowers during great vigils; Aztec farmers requested a bountiful harvest by addressing their corn seeds before planting them; women gave thanks for maize before preparing it to eat; when a baby was born, the midwife cut the infant's umbilical cord over a cob of corn, which was ceremoniously planted. The symbol of maize permeated Aztec thought: a person who achieved honour was said to have *"reached the season of the green maize ear"*.

When the Spanish arrived in Mexico in the sixteenth century, the culinary habits of the locals were a culture shock. Accustomed as they were to a European diet based on wheat, they were intrigued by maize. Without it the conquest of Mexico may never have taken place. Maize sustained Cortés and all his men throughout their mission. On several occasions local people provided them with women to grind their corn and make them *tortillas*. The leaves of the maize plant also provided fodder for their horses, the wild beasts that had so impressed the Aztecs.

Although the Spanish introduced wheat to Mexico, a crop that came to symbolise European domination, maize continued to be the staple crop in Colonial Mexico, much as it is today. The missionaries soon discovered that maize had a vital role to play in the conversion of the indigenous people to Christianity. The friars had seen local people shape images of their gods from maize, so they instructed them to form the image of Christ. Thus the sacred Aztec crop became the body of Christ. The Spanish friars believed that they had succeeded in their religious conquest. However, in many indigenous communities today, Christian and pre-Hispanic beliefs have fused to the extent that it is not easy to say whether one religion dominates the other.

This ancient ceramic dog from Colima holds a maize cob in his mouth. Dogs guided the souls of the dead to the the afterlife and ensured the future growth of maize.

The Maya people of Zinacantan in Chiapas still use the same ancient methods employed by their forefathers to plant, weed and harvest their corn. Piles of harvested maize are often topped by small wooden crosses. They call their miracle crop *sunbeam of the gods* and believe that it has an inner soul. A special ceremony is performed to the *Lord of the Earth* at the time of its planting, for it is he who sends the clouds and the rain. In this and many other indigenous communities maize is as revered today as it was in the ancient world.

In the modern world, genetically modified (GM) maize, developed by Western scientists, is the cause for much debate. Varieties of GM maize produce their own insecticides or toxins. These are harmful to wildlife such as the Monarch butterfly and contamination has now occurred in Mexico, the place of origin of the crop. Aside from the environmental impact, some Mexican companies now face difficulties developing products for export because they cannot guarantee that the maize they use is GM free.

The Aztecs would perhaps be proud today to see how many people in the world benefit from the gift of maize, but saddened to see how their gift has been commercialised for corporate interests. This is an issue of great concern for Mexican people today. The United States of America is currently the world's biggest producer and exporter of maize. More than 50% of the global maize production is consumed in the USA, about 70% of which is used to feed livestock. Maize also has a host of commercial and industrial uses, ranging from drugs and cosmetics to ethanol fuel, detergents and biodegradable plastics. Extract from the germ is used to produce cooking oil, cornstarch is used as a thickener, and corn syrup has replaced sugar in many consumable products.

Maize the provider of daily nourishment

The ancient Mexican diet was based on maize, a staple used for a variety of foods, most of which are still prepared. The protagonist was the *tortilla*, a kind of maize pancake, which provided people with their daily bread. *Tamales*, which were made of maize dough steamed in husks of corn, with a variety of fillings, were usually prepared on feast days. *Atole* was a kind of maize porridge, and maize dough was an ingredient in a chocolate beverage. Corn on the cob was boiled and roasted. Boiled corn kernels were used in a soup called *pozole*, which is still popular today. Dry kernels were used to make popcorn. The Aztecs are credited with inventing this snack, which many Europeans believe is a modern invention. The Aztecs also made syrup from maize and used the fibres of the plant to make tea.

Below: Spirit of Maize paper cut from San Pablito, Puebla. By Benito Zósimo.

Sopa de elote y chiles poblanos
Sweet corn and poblano chile soup

In Mexico you can buy fresh sweet corn in bags from the market, kernels ready removed from the cob. This corn is very tender and makes delicious soup. If you grow your own corn, remove the kernels with a knife before you cook it. As fresh corn is not available all year round in the United Kingdom and can be expensive, you can also use frozen or tinned corn. However this is less tender and may need to be sieved after boiling if you do not like the texture.

Ingredients:
500 grams sweet corn
2 tomatoes blanched and chopped
2 *poblano chiles* toasted and cut into strips or small squares
Fresh coriander (small bunch) chopped with stems removed
1 small onion chopped
2 garlic cloves crushed
1 litre chicken or vegetable stock
½ litre milk
Corn or vegetable oil for frying
Salt to taste

Preparation:
Boil the sweet corn with the chicken or vegetable stock. Leave to cool, then puree to a texture you like (finely pureed to coarse). Sieve and discard the outer skin if you prefer. Frozen and tinned corn has tougher skin. Set the puree aside.

Heat the oil in a large pan and fry the garlic and onions until soft and transparent. Add the chopped tomatoes and fry for about 3 more minutes. Put in the coriander and *poblano chiles* and cook for a further two minutes, stirring to mix the flavours. Add the sweet corn mixture and bring to the boil over low heat. When you are ready to serve the soup, add the milk and bring to the boil.

As this soup is quite time consuming to prepare, I often make a large quantity of the sweet corn mixture and freeze it (without the milk) ready to add the tomato and *chile* sauce when I need the soup.

Tortillas

A *tortilla* is a flat, thin disc or 'pancake' made traditionally from maize dough and cooked on a *comal* or griddle. *Tortillas* were eaten daily in ancient Mexico, just as they are today, with beans, squash, *chile*, tomato sauces and sometimes meat.

The history of the tortilla

The *tortilla* is probably as old as the history of maize cultivation itself, perhaps dating back to the time when corn was still a wild grass and its dry kernels or *tlayolli* were ground for consumption. The Aztec or *nahuatl* word for *tortilla* was *tlax-calli* or 'that which is boiled or cooked'. Similarly, the *tlaxcalchiquihuite* was the name of the basket the cooked *tortillas* were placed in to keep them warm. The Aztecs were accustomed to many kinds of *tortillas*, which came in different sizes, textures, thicknesses and colours (white, yellow, red or blue-green depending on the corn).

Above: basket of freshly made *tortillas*, wrapped in a cloth to keep them warm.

Everyone in the Aztec empire was entitled to a daily provision of *tortillas* (although there would of course have been additional sources of food). This we know from a description in the Aztec Codex Mendoza. Babies and toddlers were given half a *tortilla*. At four or five years of age the amount increased to a whole *tortilla* and from six to adolescence, one and a half *tortillas*. An adult was entitled to two *tortillas* as a basic minimum. These would probably have been large (about 20cm in diameter) and were made at home or purchased from in the market.

The Spanish named these maize pancakes *tortillas* or 'little cakes' from the word *torta* or cake. In Spain today, the word *tortilla* has quite a different meaning. It is used to describe a potato omelette. A Spanish omelette in Mexico is called a *tortilla española*.

Nowadays, particularly in rural communities, *tortillas* are still shaped in the palm of the hand, as they were in ancient times. This takes a lot of practice. I have never succeeded in making a round *tortilla* with this method, more an amoeba shaped variety! Although there is more work

invloved, there is nothing to equal the taste of a hot, fresh *tortilla*, made entirely of corn ground by hand on the *metate*.

Temalacatzingo, Guerrero State

In the village of Temalacatzingo in Guerrero, I once watched a young woman named Rosa grinding corn on her *metate*. She spoke to me in Spanish, but her mother spoke only nahuatl, the language of the Aztecs. This elderly lady was in fact the first native speaker of nahuatl I had heard pronounce my middle name *Xochitl*, which means 'flower' in nahuatl.

In Temalacatzingo, maize is planted, harvested and stored in the traditional way in the *cuexcomate* or grain store. As her baby lay asleep in the hammock beside her, Rosa knelt before her *metate*. Her strong arms maintained a hypnotic rhythm as she worked the corn, the rough grinding of the *metate* hand resonating around us. Pausing for a moment, as if she had felt my gaze, she pointed to a bucket of water where I could wash my hands. I had been recruited! She gestured towards the *metate*, and I took her place. Soon I had an audience. Her children had stopped their play to watch *la güera* (the fair girl) grinding corn. It was no easy job. I felt I was grinding up more of the *metate* than the corn and my movements were awkward and jolted. My feelings of inadequacy were heightened when her baby started to cry, as if

unsettled by the interruption of her mother's movements.

I handed back the *mano*, and admitted that grinding corn was hard work. "Not when you have plenty of practise," she replied, giggling at my sudden loss of enthusiasm. "Besides, I like to be close to my animals and see my children playing. Here I can watch them while I work."

Maize in the Modern World

A popular alternative to grinding corn by hand is to use packaged *masa harina* flour (now widely available outside Mexico). *Masa harina* or maize flour is not the same as corn flour in the United Kingdom. *Masa harina* is produced through a process known as *nixtamalization,* in which the maize kernels are soaked in lime (*cal* or *tequesquite*). This makes the corn easier to grind, kills off toxins and helps to preserve the dough. The process also increases the protein and nutrient value of the corn. *Nixtamalization,* practised all over Mexico today, is a process archaeologists date back to around 1500 BC.

Today millions of *tortillas* in Mexico are produced by machine. It is a common sight to see people visit the *tortilleria* to purchase, by weight, a supply of freshly made *tortillas,* in the same way that one would visit a bakery for bread in other countries. While much of the flavour and tradition is lost in the machine made variety, the industrialization of *tortillas* in Mexico makes them accessible to all in the modern world. Most people do not have time to make them, any more than we have time to grind wheat and make our own daily bread. However, there are instances when technology and tradition blend. We have met people at *tortillerias* in villages who take along maize they have grown themselves, ready boiled, to be made into dough by machine. Then they take the dough back home to make their own *tortillas,* thus maintaining the flavour of the homegrown maize, but eliminating some of the work. People in Mexico are very good at making the most of local resources. They also take their turkeys to the bakery at Christmas time to make use of the large ovens (as I discovered when I went to buy a loaf of bread!)

I once spent a whole day at a *tortilleria* marvelling at the *tortilla* making process. First the maize is soaked in alkaline water (lime) overnight and rinsed. Then it is boiled and put through a mill to be ground into dough. The dough is placed on a funnel and passes through round cutters (similar to when pasta is made). Out come the uncooked *tortillas* onto a conveyor belt, which is heated underneath. At some point they are miraculously flipped over and reappear cooked at the other end, dropping efficiently into a neat pile. We once bought an ingenious looking devise, a work top *tortilla* maker will two heavy rollers and cutters, but we have never managed to get this to work!

The *tortillas* you find in most British supermarkets are very distant relatives of those prepared in Mexico. The commercial, packaged variety is usually made of wheat flour, as wheat is easier to preserve (wheat *tortillas* are found in many parts of Mexico, but are more common in the North where wheat is grown). Maize *tortillas* do not have a long shelf life, which is why you can only buy them from specialists frozen. Do not judge *tortillas* on the packaged variety if you have never experience the real thing. There is no comparison! Unfortunately there are no *tortillerias* selling freshly made *tortillas* in the United Kingdom, but you can make them yourself with *masa harina* and a metal or wooden *tortilla* press. It does not take long to make them for family and friends and is well worth the effort.

Como hacer masa
How to make masa (maize dough)

Masa harina is maize flour made from corn which has been soaked in alkaline water. It is used for making *tortillas* and other maize based dishes. *Maseca,* the most popular brand, is available through specialist stockists.

Ingredients:
275 grams of *masa-harina* flour (Maseca)
350 ml warm water
Salt

Preparation:
Place the *masa* flour in a bowl. Work in warm water with your fingers and knead for about 5 minutes to make soft dough. If the dough is crumbly or dry, add a little more water. Shape the dough into a large ball and cover with a damp tea towel to prevent from drying out.

Using masa:
In Mexico *masa* is used mainly for making *tortillas* (flat, thin discs or 'pancakes') however it is also used for making *tamales* (steamed maize dough wrapped in corn husks), *sopes* (thick corn cakes with raised edges), *gordas* (fat *tortillas* with a filling inserted), *empanadas* (pies or turnovers), *atole* (a beverage) and many *botanas* (appetizers). Instructions for some of these foods are provided later in this chapter.

Como hacer tortillas de maiz
How to make maize tortillas

You will need some essential tools:

A *tortilla press*, to shape the *tortillas*

A *comal* or griddle, on which to cook the *tortillas*

Two pieces of plastic for lining the *tortilla press* (a freezer bag cut out is perfect)

Masa-harina flour or *Maseca* (maize flour prepared especially for making *tortillas* and other maize based dishes)

Ingredients:

275 grams *Masa-harina (Maseca)*

350 ml warm water

Salt

This makes about 22 to 25 small *tortillas*

(small *tortillas* are best for *tacos*)

Preparation:

Place the *masa* flour in a bowl. Work in warm water with your fingers and knead for about 5 minutes to make soft dough. If the dough is crumbly or dry, add a little more water. Shape the dough into a large ball and cover with a damp tea towel to prevent from drying out.

Pre-heat an ungreased *comal* or griddle over medium heat. A non-stick crêpe pan is also very good for the job. The *comal* is ready when a drop of water appears to dance on it. Shape a piece of dough roughly the size of a walnut and place on the lined *tortilla press*, slightly off centre away from the handle. Press the ball of dough slightly to flatten it.

Place another piece of plastic on top of the dough. Close the *tortilla* press firmly and open. Peel the plastic from the top and bottom of the flat *tortilla*. Place the *tortilla* on the hot *comal* and cook for 15-20 seconds. The colour changes slightly as the *tortilla* cooks. Turn over and cook for 20 seconds, turn again for 10-15 seconds and pat the *tortilla* with a spatula (wooden or plastic). The *tortilla* should puff up when it is ready. This is usually a sign that the *tortillas* are cooked, but do not worry if this does not happen. Stack and wrap the *tortillas* in a dry cotton tea towel once they are ready.

If you cannot get a *tortilla* as thin as you would like it, this is because the dough needs more moisture, not because you have not pressed the *tortilla press* hard enough. Wet your hand with water or sprinkle some onto the dough and try again until you get the correct result. Remember that there is an art to making *tortillas* and your skills will improve with practise. Take some comfort in the fact that the majority of Mexicans we have met in the United Kingdom do not know how to make *tortillas; t*hey are so used to buying them!

If you make more *tortillas* than you need, you can keep them for another day by placing them in a dry cloth inside a plastic bag in the fridge. They can then be re-heated in a cloth in the microwave oven for 40 seconds in groups of 10-12. They can also be re-heated on the griddle one by one as when you made them. If any of the *tortillas* have become very dry, run under a tap and place on the griddle.

The first couple of *tortillas* you make will not be perfect. The griddle needs to be properly heated and you will need time for warming up your skills! These first *tortillas,* and any others that end up in the 'reject pile' need not be wasted. Make yourself some *quesadillas* while you are cooking (*tortillas* with a melted cheese filling) or eat them as they are with a little salt and whatever takes your fancy.

Using tortillas

When *tortillas* are freshly made, they are best used for *tacos* or *quesadillas* (*tortillas* filled with cheese). A basket of fresh *tortillas* can accompany any meal (as bread does on the Continent). There are so many things you can do with *tortillas* and old ones never go to waste. They can be used for making *huevos rancheros* (Ranch-style eggs), *enchiladas* (rolled *tortillas* in a *chile* sauce), *tostadas* (fried *tortillas* with toppings), *flautas* (rolled fried *tacos*) and *totopos* (*tortilla* chips) to name a few. If you have just embarked on your *tortilla*-making career, you may want to start off by making something simple with them. *Quesadillas* are delicious and easy to make.

Quesadillas
Cheese-filled tortillas

Quesadillas are the kind of snack you make when everyone is hovering in the kitchen. They are fun and informal. If you come home hungry from a late night out, *quesadillas* can be made in a couple of minutes, provided you have a few *tortillas* and some cheese in the fridge.

Ingredients:
Tortillas
Cheese, grated or sliced (Cheddar or any cheese that melts)

Preparation:
Heat a couple of *tortillas* on a griddle or large frying pan, and arrange a little cheese in the middle of them (not too much or you will end up with a sticky mess!) Then fold each *tortilla* in half with a spatula and your fingers (take care not to burn yourself). Pat down your *quesadilla* with your spatula, until the cheese starts to melt. This will prevent the *tortilla* from springing open again. Turn over and leave until the cheese is well melted. Serve immediately (*quesadillas* are made to be eaten straight away). Mexicans will invariably add *chile* or *salsa*.

In Mexico *quesadillas* are also made with ham, courgette flowers and other ingredients, though they all contain cheese. The word *quesadilla* is a combination of the Spanish for cheese (queso) and *tortilla*. Add whatever ingredients take your fancy, but take care not to overload the *quesadilla*.

The Authentic Mexican *Taco*

When you become more skilled at making *tortillas*, you can use them for making *tacos*, a word you may be confused about, unless you have actually been in Mexico. Tex-Mex restaurants and many supermarkets in the United Kingdom sell 'taco shells' and kits, which are usually an American creation. Most Mexicans would not recognise them, nor would they appreciate the excess of *chile* powder in the fillings that go with them. I once saw a Mexican musician in London trying to eat a *taco* shell. He looked at it somewhat suspiciously, then endeavoured to take a bite. At this point most of the runny mince (which he clearly did not recognise either) spilled out the other end and the shell fell apart. His well pressed white cotton outfit was in the firing line, so he gave up and ordered a hot dog instead. To be honest, I would rather eat the filling on its own.

A *taco* is simply a *tortilla* rolled up with a filling. The name given to different kinds of *tacos* in Mexico depends on the region, how they are prepared and the ingredients used. There are seemingly endless varieties.

Tacos de canasta or 'basket' *tacos* are 'morning' *tacos* prepared by vendors at home, wrapped in paper and sold in the street from the basket. *Tacos al carbon*, also called *tacos de carne asada*, are made with marinated meat cooked on a grill. *Tacos al pastor* which means literally 'shepherd's style *tacos'* are a variation of Middle-Eastern spit-grilled meat, introduced by immigrants from Lebanon. They are made with marinated pork and cooked on a rotisserie with a pineapple on top. *Tacos de carnitas* are made with pork cooked in lard with orange rind, which gives them a distinctive golden brown colour. Here every imaginable part of the pig is creatively put to use and most Mexicans have their favourite 'part'. Similarly *tacos de cabeza* are made with different parts of the cow. *Tacos de barbacoa* or 'barbecue style' are generally made from a whole lamb baked in the ground in a bed of roasted maguey leaves. *Tacos de fritangas* are made with fried meat and *tacos de cazuela* are prepared with any filling cooked in a pot. *Tacos de pescado* are fish *tacos* and *flautas* or *tacos*

dorados are fried *tacos*. There are an exotic variety of *tacos indigenas* (indigenous *tacos*) made with insects and caviar amongst other things. Almost anything that can be rolled inside a *tortilla* can become a *taco*, so you are at liberty to invent your own!

Tacos are enjoyed all over Mexico. At the best *taco* stands you will see people from all walks of life rub shoulders. In this sense *tacos* are great levellers and an intrinsic part of what it means to be Mexican. *Tacos* are served in many restaurants in Mexico, including the most sophisticated. However, as any Mexican will tell you, the best *tacos* in town are usually to be found at *puestos* (stands) or at the more permanent *taquerias*. Except in restaurants, *tacos* are usually eaten standing.

Taco stands are usually carts fully equipped with everything needed to prepare whatever type of *taco* is on offer. For *tacos de bistek*, for example, this 'kitchen on wheels' usually consists of a large curved cooking area where meat, onions and *tortillas* are fried, heated by gas burners below. To one side is a wooden block where meat and vegetables are finely chopped.

The usual procedure is to ask for *una orden*, an order of *tacos*, how many depends on the size and type on offer. You will be asked how many you want "*¿cuantas?*". For my favourite, *tacos al pastor*, this usually means four or five if they are small. These *tacos* are served with garnish and *chile* (the amount is to taste and you are usually asked first). No one would ever encourage you to have *chile*, but if you are a foreigner with a liking for the sauce, there will be knowing smiles all around!

Taco stands are usually crowded so you will be served one round. While you are busy eating away, other people will be served. As you approach your last *taco*, you place your order for another round. An experienced *taco* vendor will anticipate your preferences before you finish, and will skilfully juggle a large number of orders. How many you eat is entirely up to you, but in my experience the eyes are usually bigger than the stomach. You are often served on

brightly coloured plastic plates lined with a piece of grease-proof paper. This is discarded ready for use for the next customer. You pay for the number of *tacos* you have eaten before you leave. There is a certain amount of 'taco etiquette' involved. I have never seen anyone jump the queue (as people are always doing in China) and ordering as many *tacos* as you think you can eat is not the done thing. I once ordered ten and the polite vendor suggested diplomatically that I started with three or four. There is no point having a pile of *tacos* on your plate getting cold, especially when there are other hungry mouths to feed. You can also order *tacos* to take home.

The instructions on how to prepare *tacos* in this book, are presented courtesy of Rafa in the village of Tonalá, Jalisco. He generously shared his knowledge on the subject, once he was sure that we were not going to represent any likely competition!

I have spent many happy hours with Mexican friends in the United Kingdom discussing Mexican cuisine. At all our gatherings, the conversation inevitably turns to food! High on the wish list of many homesick Mexicans is an order of real *tacos* (not the anglicised version). If they could open the door and find a *taco* stand on the street corner, it would be a wish come true. The likelihood of that happening on a cold, rainy winter's day is fairly slim, but the good news is that it is possible to make *tacos* yourself. *Taco* parties are fun and they need not mean a lot of preparation. You can improvise with the fillings or even use your Sunday leftovers. Once you have tasted the real thing, you will never be tempted by a *taco* shell again!

When *tacos* are chosen from the menu at our restaurant, we show our guests how to eat them the Mexican way. We bring a basket of freshly made hot *tortillas* to the table and fillings of different kinds. Then each person makes his or her own *taco*.

How to make a *taco*:
A guide for the uninitiated foreigner

Open the basket, unfold the cloth and take a *tortilla* in one hand. Be careful, as they may be hot (always fold the cloth up again or the other *tortillas* will get cold). Hold the flat *tortilla* in the palm of one hand and spoon on a small amount of filling, with the aid of a fork or spoon. There are usually a variety of fillings on the table and discovering which ones and how much make a delicious combination takes practise. I would recommend a thin spreading of refried beans and a meat or vegetable filling, topped with a little *guacamole, salsa,* cheese and creme frâiche. Fold your *tortilla* around the filling (like a cigar) and eat each one, as it is prepared.

Do not overload your *taco*; to Mexicans this looks greedy. A *taco* is not a *kebab* and filling it like one will make it impossible to roll up or fold. If you overfill your *tortilla* it will probably disintegrate before your very eyes. Left to their own devices, some of our customers fill one *tortilla* with half the filling in the bowl, start piling quantities of filling onto their plates, hog all the cream, or eat their *tacos* with a knife and fork. But not for long if my mother is watching!

Remember that you can eat as many *tacos* as you like, and a fresh supply of *tortillas* will be constantly available. It is much better to eat more *tacos* with less filling than a few to bursting point. Mexicans like to take their time over food. For some reason many of our British guests seem to be in a tremendous hurry, as if anything not already on their plate will be taken away from them! We have observed that those who rush tend to eat less overall whereas those who linger and take breaks for conversation, enjoy and consume a great deal more. One thing for sure is that no one is left feeling hungry.

A *Taco* Meal or *Taco* Party

There are many different fillings for *tacos*. Unless you are organising a party, you are unlikely to prepare more than one basic meat or vegetable filling for your *tacos* and these can be prepared in advance and frozen. *Salsa* and *guacamole* should be freshly made (though you can chop the ingredients in advance). Toppings like crème frâiche require no preparation at all.

Suggested fillings for a *taco* meal:

Meat or vegetable fillings
Fresh *salsas*
Guacamole
Refried beans
Crème frâiche

We provide the following meat and vegetable fillings in our restaurant for *taco* parties. The vegetable fillings are not prepared specially for vegetarians and will be enjoyed by all:

Chicken *taco* filling
Beef *taco* filling
Courgettes with sweet corn
Potato and *poblano chile* filling
Poblano chiles with cheese and cream

Relleno de pollo para tacos

Chicken filling for tacos and pasta

Ingredients:

300 to 400 grams chicken cooked and shredded
(the filling can also be made with any left over roasted meat)
1 onion chopped
1 or 2 tomatoes blanched and chopped
1 or 2 tinned *jalapeño chiles* chopped
1 garlic clove
1 tablespoon corn or vegetable oil
1 teaspoon of pepper
Ground cumin to taste
½ teaspoon salt

Preparation:

Crush the garlic with the salt to form a paste. Heat the oil in a large heavy frying pan. Add onion and garlic paste. Cook until the onion is tender. Add tomatoes, *chiles*, pepper and cumin. Stir in the chicken. Continue to cook and stir until the mixture is fairly dry. Add more salt and cumin to taste.

Cook's tip: I often boil a whole chicken and prepare quantities of filling for the freezer, packing it in 500 gram containers. It can also be used for improvising quick tasty pasta dishes. Pasta is popular in Mexico, but is used differently. It is served in smaller portions as a starter.

For pasta:

250 grams pasta
500 grams ready made chicken filling
250 grams crème frâiche
Cheddar cheese grated

Preparation:

Boil the pasta (following manufacturer's instructions). Drain and place in an ovenproof dish. Add 250 grams of crème frâiche, the ready prepared chicken and grated cheese. Mix well with the aid of a fork. Place in a hot oven for 10 minutes or until bubbling and serve with a green salad and French bread. The dish can be heated through in the microwave.

Relleno de res para tacos
Shredded beef filling for tacos

Ingredients for cooking the meat:
450 grams or 1lb boneless beef chuck (ask your butcher for this cut as it shreds well)
Water (enough to cover the meat)
½ small onion
6 peppercorns
Salt

Ingredients for the filling:
2 small tomatoes blanched and chopped
½ onion chopped
1 garlic clove
1 tablespoon corn or vegetable oil
¼ teaspoon ground cumin
Freshly ground pepper
Salt

Preparing the meat:
Place the meat in a large saucepan and add the water, peppercorns, onion and salt to taste. Bring to the boil, then reduce the heat, covering and simmering until the meat is very tender (for about 1-1 ½ hours). Cool the meat in its broth. (The broth will keep the meat moist and preserve the flavour). Drain the meat and keep the broth for making a tasty soup. If you use this recipe with any other beef cut that is less tender, boil for two hours or more. Chuck is used in Mexico because it shreds well and is more economical.

Preparing the filling:
Shred the meat with the aid of two forks. Mash the garlic with ¼ teaspoon of salt to make a paste. Heat the oil in a large frying pan and add the chopped onion and garlic paste. Cook until the onion is tender. Cut the *chiles* into short strips. Add the *chile* and tomatoes to the cooked onions. Cook for 3 to 4 minutes. Add the meat, cumin and freshly ground pepper to taste. Cook until the meat is heated through, stirring in broth for moisture. Season to taste. Serve the filling hot for *tacos*.

Relleno de papas con chiles poblanos
Potato and poblano chile filling for tacos

Ingredients:
2 or more potatoes boiled in their skin
1 small onion, finely chopped
1 garlic clove crushed or chopped
1 *poblano chile*, toasted, skin removed and finely chopped
Salt to taste
Corn or vegetable oil for frying

Preparation:
Remove the skin from the boiled potatoes, then grate or dice them. Heat some oil in a frying pan and fry the onion and garlic until soft and transparent. Add the potato, blend with the onion and garlic and stir in the *poblano chile*. Season with salt to taste.

Relleno de calabacitas con elote
Courgette and sweet corn filling for tacos

Ingredients:
1 or 2 courgettes, par boiled whole and diced
½ mug cooked sweet corn
2 tomatoes blanched and chopped (juice and pips removed)
1 onion finely chopped
1 garlic clove crushed or finely chopped
Jalapeño or *poblano chiles* finely chopped (optional)
Fresh or dried herbs
Salt to taste
Corn or vegetable oil for frying

Preparation:
Heat some oil in a frying pan and fry the onion and garlic. Add the tomatoes and fry for about 3 minutes, then the courgettes, sweet corn, *chiles* if used and herbs. Season with salt to taste.

Enchiladas and enjitomatadas

Tortillas have many uses in Mexican cooking and are never thrown away. When fresh we use them to make delicious *tacos*. When not fresh, we cut them in triangles and make *totopos* (*tortilla* chips). We make *tortillas* cut in strips into *chilaquiles*.

Enchiladas, *enjitomatadas* and *enfrijoladas* are other dishes which use *tortillas*. *Enchiladas* are made with *tortillas* dipped in a hot *chile* sauce, *enjitomatadas* in a tomato sauce, and *enfrijoladas* in bean sauce.

Enchiladas

Ingredients for the sauce:
6 *ancho chiles*
1 *pasilla chile*
1 garlic clove
¼ onion
Salt

Preparing the sauce:
Always use disposable vinyl gloves when handling *chiles*.
Wash the *chiles* and remove the seeds and stalk. Heat a spoon of oil in a frying pan and toast the *chiles* lightly. Place the *chiles* in a bowl, pour boiling water over them and leave to soak for 30 minutes. Puree the *chiles* with the onion and garlic using some of the water in which they were soaked. Sieve the mixture. A friend of ours did this without placing a bowl underneath the sieve. Her precious sauce went down the sink and she was left with the worthless pulp. Remember your bowl!

Heat some oil in a saucepan and fry the pureed mixture, adding some chicken or vegetable stock if needed. Simmer for 15 minutes, stirring so the mixture does not stick to the pan. This is the basic sauce for *enchiladas*. It keeps well in the fridge for a long time.

Ingredients for the *enchiladas*:
Maize *tortillas*
Chicken cooked and shredded
Crème fraîche
Cheddar cheese
Corn or vegetable oil for frying
Salt

For garnish:
Onion sliced
Lettuce shredded

Preparing the *enchiladas*:
Fry the *tortillas* lightly on both sides in a shallow frying pan (to seal them). Dip the *tortillas* in the *chile* sauce while hot and place in a warm dish. Place the shredded chicken on the *tortilla* and roll into a flute. Repeat with the other *tortillas* and place in a dish. Pour over the rest of the *chile* sauce and add the crème fraîche and cheese (place in the oven if not to be eaten immediately). Garnish with shredded lettuce and sliced onion.

Different varieties of *enchiladas*

There are many different kinds of *enchiladas* in Mexico. *Enchiladas suizas* (Swiss *enchiladas*) are so called because they are made with cream and cheese. *Enchiladas verdes* (green *enchiladas*) are made with any green sauce. This may be made with *tomatillos* (green tomatoes), green *chiles*, *poblano chile* sauce or *pepián* sauce. *Enchiladas rojas* (red *enchiladas*) are made with any red sauce such as *ancho chile* and tomato. *Enchiladas de mole* are simply *enchiladas* made with *mole* sauce. The possibilities are endless and this is just the sauce! *Enchiladas* are usually filled with chicken but we have seen some with beef or vegetables. It is not uncommon to see a restaurant menu offering *enchiladas de lo que usted quiere* (*enchiladas* made with whatever you want)!

Enjitomatadas

Ingredients for the sauce:
6 *tortillas* (3 per person)
6 tomatoes
1 small onion
Clove of garlic
Coriander, or any other herb that you like
1 *jalapeño chile*
1 chicken breast cooked and shredded (reserve stock)
Chicken stock
Crème frâiche
Cheddar cheese (or any cheese that melts)

For garnish:
Lettuce shredded
Onion finely sliced

Preparing the sauce:
Puree the tomatoes, coriander, onion, garlic and *chile* with the chicken stock. Heat some oil in a saucepan, add the puree and cook the sauce for about five minutes.

Preparing the enjitomatadas:
Fry the *tortillas* lightly on both sides in a shallow frying pan (to seal them). Dip the *tortillas* in the tomato sauce while hot and place in a warm dish. Place the shredded chicken on the *tortilla* and roll into a flute. Repeat with the other *tortillas* and place in a dish. Pour over the rest of the tomato sauce and add the crème frâiche and cheese (place in the oven if not to be eaten immediately). Garnish with shredded lettuce and sliced onion.

Tostadas

A *tostada* is a fried, crispy *tortilla* with a topping. Precious *tortillas* that have had their day are ideal for making into *tostadas*, as once they are fried they are transformed. The best *tostadas* I remember eating were in a village called San Bartolo Coyotepec in Oaxaca, on a trip with Anna. The *tostadas* were delicious and it was good to have a travel companion to share the experience with. This village is famous for its striking black pottery.

To make a *tostada* you need:
Tortillas
Cooked chicken shredded
Refried beans
Avocado sliced
Tomato sliced
Pickled *jalapeño chiles* sliced
Lettuce shredded
Crème frâiche
Wenslydale cheese crumbled

Preparation:
Shallow fry the *tortillas*, one at a time, on both sides until golden and crispy. Remove any excess oil with a paper towel. Spread the tostadas with refried beans and crème frâiche. Top with shredded chicken, avocado, tomato and *chile* sliced. Add shredded lettuce and top with crumbled cheese.

How to eat a *tostada*:
Always eat *tostadas* cold with your hands. There is an art to this! Hold the *tostada* with both hands, keeping horizontal and raise to your mouth carefully. Take small bites. The *tostadas* we have tried in Mexican restaurants in the United Kingdom have been soggy, overfilled and swamped in melted cheddar cheese. This makes them sticky and impossible to eat. They should be fresh and crisp. The order you place the ingredients onto the *tostada* is important. Beans are spread on easily first, followed by the cream. If the cream goes on the lettuce at the end, it can get up your nose!

Totopos
Tortilla chips

If you have any old left over *tortillas*, they can be made into *totopos* (*tortilla* chips). Nothing goes to waste in Mexico. *Tortilla* chips are popular in Britain and are sold in a variety of flavours. In Mexico there is only one traditional kind, the freshly made kind. The variety comes with what you eat them with. You will often find *totopos* on your table when you sit down to eat in a restaurant. They are dipped into *salsas*, *guacamole* and refried beans. *Nachos* (*tortilla* chips with melted cheese and *salsa*) are actually an American invention. Mexicans prefer a range of *salsas* to dip into. The nearest equivalent is *chilaquiles* (*tortilla* chips with a tomato and *chile* sauce).

To make *totopos*, simply cut *tortillas* in quarters and then cut the quarters in half again (this is the best shape for 'dipping' into *salsas*). Deep fry the *totopos*, a small handful at a time, in hot oil. They should sizzle at once. When slightly brown, remove at once with a skimmer. Drain on a paper towel and when cool add salt.

Chilaquiles

Chilaquiles are the nearest Mexican equivalent to *nachos* and are made with fried *totopos* and a tomato and *chile* sauce. You will need about 12 *tortillas* for 600 ml of sauce. Boil the sauce in a saucepan and then add the *totopos*. Leave for a few minutes until much of the water evaporates and the *totopos* have absorbed the *salsa*. Then arrange the *totopos* on a plate. If you like, garnish with finely chopped onion, crème fraîche and crumbled Wensleydale or grated cheddar cheese. Some people bake their *chilaquiles* in the oven for about 20 minutes until the cheese melts. You can also add chicken for a light meal.

Old *tortillas*, cut in triangles are also delicious with scrambled egg. Fry the *tortilla* pieces first with a little oil. When crispy, add the egg (beaten) and mix together until cooked.

Other uses for *masa* or maize dough

Once you become accustomed to using *masa* or maize dough, you will discover that it has many other uses. Try making these *botanas* or appetizers.

Empanadas
Small 'pasties' or turnovers

Ingredients:
½ kilo of *masa*
3 tablespoons wheat flour (for elasticity only - omit for gluten-free)
1 onion chopped
1 *jalapeño chile* chopped
Fetta cheese
Epazote or any other herb you prefer
Salt
Corn or vegetable oil for frying

Preparation:
Make the *masa* following the instructions *How to make maize tortillas*. Cover with a plastic bag. Make *tortillas* with a *tortilla* press. They should be thicker for *empanadas* as they are going to be fried (use a couple of tablespoons less of water when making the dough). As you make each *tortilla*, fill with a little cheese, onion, *chile* and *epazote* or herbs of your choice. Fold the *tortilla* in half, and press down the edges to seal. When all the *empanadas* are made, fry them on both sides in a shallow frying pan in hot oil until golden. To serve as a *botana*, place a bowl of *salsa* in the middle of a large plate and arrange the *empanadas* around it.

You can use many different fillings for *empanadas*.

Molotes
Maize fritters

Molotes are an excellent *botana* or appetizer. I learnt to make them at my friend Lupita's restaurant *'Nu-Luu'* in Oaxaca, one of the most relaxing places I have visited in Mexico.

Ingredients:
½ kilo *masa*
A handful of wheat flour
Chorizo sausage (the Spanish type is readily available in most supermarkets)
3 medium sized potatoes (boiled in their skin, peeled and chopped or grated)
1 tablespoon of lard
Salt to taste
Corn or vegetable oil for frying

Preparation:
Make the *masa* following the instructions for making *tortillas*, cover with a plastic bag and set aside. Remove the skin of the chorizo and cut the sausage into pieces. Fry in a pan to bring out the juices. Add the potatoes and toss together for a few minutes.

Mix the *masa* with the lard and flour and a little salt. Make a very small *tortilla* (not too thin) using a *tortilla* press. Place the *tortilla* in the palm of your hand and add a teaspoon of potato mixture. Cup your palm and use your other hand to roll the *tortilla* up like a cigar, sealing the ends. Do not worry if you find this difficult. It took me a long time to get the hang of it! Once all the *molotes* are prepared, deep fry them in hot vegetable oil until golden.

For vegetarians, use vegetarian lard and substitute the *chorizo* for toasted *poblano chiles* or peppers. I find that *molotes* freeze very well. Leave them to cool first, and then place them on a tray and open freeze. Once frozen put the *molotes* in a plastic bag loose. Defreeze them when needed. Deep-fry them for a minute or so and they will be as delicious as freshly made ones. Serve with *guacamole*.

Atole de frutas
Fruit atole

Atole is an appetizing maize beverage, made in a variety of flavours and often served with *tamales*. It is a common sight in the evenings in Mexico to see women *atole* sellers take their places in town squares and street corners, offering this delicious beverage to passers by.

Ingredients:
125 grams *masa harina*
2 litres water
2 kilos of pineapple, *guava* or another seasonal fruit
1 cinnamon stick
125 grams sugar
The peel of an orange

Preparation:
Cook the fruit with the sugar and 1½ litres of the water until tender. Puree when cool. Mix the *masa harina* with the rest of the water and add to the fruit. Add the orange peel and bring to the boil. Add water to taste.

Atole de pepitas
Pumpkin seed atole

Ingredients:
500 grams maize
500 grams pumpkin seeds
500 grams sugar
2 ½ litres Water

Preparation:
Boil the maize and pumpkin seeds in plenty of water until they are soft. Drain and puree in a blender, then sieve. Boil 2 ½ litres of water in a saucepan. Add the pureed maize and pumpkin seeds and when the mixture begins to thicken, add the sugar. Stir continuously while heating.

Tamales

Steamed maize dough in corn husks (basic recipe)

Ingredients:
500 grams *masa harina*
250 grams lard
Hot chicken or vegetable stock
25 sweet corn husks
1 teaspoon baking powder
Salt

To prepare the leaves:
In Mexico maize husks (fresh or dry) and banana leaves are used for making *tamales*. You can also use spinach leaves. Some Mexicans in the United Kingdom have improvised with lotus leaves available at Chinese supermarkets. Wash the leaves thoroughly, soak them and drain. If using dry cornhusks, pour boiling water over them so they regain their elasticity. Keep them moist until ready to use.

To make the *tamales*:
Whip the lard with a mixer until white and frothy. Add the hot chicken or vegetable stock and *masa harina* alternately, little by little, whipping continuously into dough. The dough is ready when a small ball of dough floats when dropped into a cup of water. With a leaf in one hand place a spoonful of dough onto the leaf, followed by any filling you like, sweet or savoury (chicken, beef, dry fruit etc). Fold the leaves around the dough and steam for two hours on a low heat.

Left: basket of tamales. Codex Mendoza.

Tamales de nuez
Nut tamales

Ingredients:
500 grams *masa harina*
250 grams lard
125 grams chopped walnuts, almonds or a mixture of both.
125 grams sugar
125 grams dried fruits; prunes, raisins, dates, etc. (optional)
25 maize husks

Preparation:
Prepare the leaves (see basic recipe).
Boil milk and sugar in a saucepan until the liquid reduces by half. Whip the lard with a mixer until white and frothy. Add the hot milk and *masa harina* alternately, little by little and continue whipping for about 5 to 6 minutes. The dough is ready when a small ball of dough floats when dropped into a cup of water. With a leaf in one hand place a spoonful of dough and nuts on the leaf. Add the dried fruits if you are using them. Fold the leaves around the dough and steam for two hours on a low heat.

Huitlacoche

Think of the most coveted mushroom known to Western cuisine and chances are the *truffle* will spring to mind. *Huitlacoche* or *cuitlacoche* is to Mexicans what the truffle is to Western chefs and is considered a delicacy. It is actually a kind of fungus that grows on the kernels of maize. *Huitlacoche* is cherished in Mexico, but in other parts of the world, where no one knows what to do with it, it is generally discarded. It makes excellent soup, *quesadillas*, *empanadas* and is delicious as a filling for crêpes. I tried them for the first time at my friend Alejandra's wedding in a beautiful hotel garden in Guanajuato.

In Mexico *huitlacoche* is more plentiful during the rain season from July to October and there is always a high demand for it. It is harvested without causing any damage to the growing ears of corn. While it is almost impossible to buy

fresh *huitlacoche* outside Mexico, it is now available in tins in the United Kingdom from the Mexican company *Herdez*, who market their products in Britain under the name *Doña Maria*.

Relleno de huitlacoche
Huitlacoche filling

The filling can be used for *quesadillas* and empanadas and for crêpes. Follow the instructions for crêpes with courgette flower filling in the chapter: *Marrow, Pumpkin and Squash.*

Ingredients:
1 tin of *huitlacoche* (440 grams)
1 chicken breast cooked and shredded (optional)
1 small onion finely chopped
1 garlic clove finely chopped
3 tablespoons chopped *epazote* or any fresh herb you like
500 grams crème frâiche
250 grams grated cheese
Corn or vegetable for frying
Salt and pepper to taste

Preparation:
Chop the *huitlacoche*. Heat the oil in a large pan with a lid and fry the onion and garlic until soft and transparent. Add the fresh herbs and *huitlacoche*, seasoned with salt and pepper, and fry for 5 minutes. Place the lid on the pan and simmer for a further 10 minutes.

Fill crêpes with the *huitlacoche* mixture and some chicken (optional). Roll up the crêpes, place them in a buttered dish and top with crème frâiche and grated cheese. Heat the dish in a hot oven for 15 to 20 minutes for the cheese to melt. Serve hot with a green salad.

Spirit of the *chile* paper cut. San Pablito, Puebla. By Benito Zósimo.

Chilli

El chile - Chilli - Capsicum

Chile, derived from the Aztec nahuatl *chilli*, is an ingredient at the heart of Mexican cuisine. In recognition of this we have used the Spanish spelling throughout this book. The majority of *chiles* belong to the *Capsicum annuum* family of plants. Astonishingly, there are some two thousand varieties, about sixty of which are in cultivation. All *chiles* are native to the Americas and the majority (about 90%) originated in Mexico.

For many people, especially in the United Kingdom, the word *chile* means just one thing: hot and spicy. For this reason opinion prevails that all Mexican food is hot, which is not the case. The majority of *chiles* in Mexico are added to food for flavour, not to test powers of endurance. There are many varieties of *chile* that are not hot. Bell peppers, for example, called *chile pimiento* in Spanish, and sweet peppers, used to make *paprika*, also belong to the *Capsicum* family and contain no capsaicin (the chemical responsible for the 'burn'). The strength of any *chile* will depend on the type of plant, where it is grown and how ripe the fruit is.

From a modern perspective it is impossible to fully appreciate the impact that the *chile* pepper has had on world cuisine. In shops today, we have a wide variety of spices with which to season our food, and in specialist shops spices can be bought from almost any country in the world. Things were very different five hundred years ago. Spices were rare and cherished commodities, for they could only be grown in specific tropical conditions. Consequently, only the privileged could afford them and the person in charge of spices in any European household was a trustworthy individual imbued with status.

In the fifteenth and sixteenth centuries, one of the great driving forces behind navel expeditions and voyages of discovery was the search for 'pepper' or spices. When

Columbus set sail towards America, he did so in search of a shorter route to the Far East, then the main source for spices. Queen Isabella of Spain even parted with her jewels to finance his expedition. The newly discovered islands Columbus reached were named *The Indies* and the inhabitants *Indians* as Columbus believed he had arrived in India. The name stuck and the word *West* was added to *Indies* to alleviate confusion. Likewise, *chiles* were called *peppers* as the Spanish had come in search of this spice and believed erroneously that they had found it.

Introduced to Europe by the Spanish in the fifteenth century, *chiles* were readily adopted and spread quickly all over the world, for unlike oriental spices, *chiles* can be cultivated in many countries. It is hard to imagine Far Eastern food without *chile*, but without this plant there would be no Indian or Sri Lankan curries. Today these are considered national dishes, though only hundreds, not thousands of years old. Interestingly, some of the most pungent Far Eastern dishes are too hot even for Mexicans to handle. At the other end of the scale, sweet peppers have been adopted enthusiastically across the Mediterranean and Hungarian cuisine has become synonymous with *paprika*, the dried powder made from sweet peppers. Tabasco sauce (named after a state in Southern Mexico), was born when a North American soldier took home a handful of *piquin chiles*. These small *chiles* still grow in the wild in Mexico today.

An Aztec man punishes his son for misbehaving, by making him inhale the smoke of roasting *chiles*. Codex Mendoza.

Chiles have been cultivated in Mexico since 3000 BC. In ancient times, *chile* played an important role in the diet of the Mexican people, just as it does today. Together with maize, squash and beans, *chile* provides a healthy, highly nutritious diet. One *chile* can contain a day's allowance of vitamin C. *Chile* is also extremely good for the digestion as it speeds up the metabolism. For this reason, appetizers and

salsas containing *chile* are usually already at the table when you sit down to a meal in a Mexican restaurant today. As well as for consumption, the Aztecs had other ingenious uses for the *chile* pepper. *Chiles* were used as a painkiller for toothache and earache and even assisted in childbirth. A skillful midwife would expose the mother to *chile* dust at a crucial moment in the delivery, thus making her sneeze, facilitating the birth. Pre-Hispanic doctors used *chile* to treat respiratory and digestive problems and mixed ground *chile*, honey and alkaline water to treat colds. Aztec children who misbehaved had to breath in the vapors of roasting *chile* peppers as punishment, as I remind my school children when I am giving classes on Aztec culture! When my mother undertakes one of her marathon *chile* roasting sessions, the effect in her kitchen is somewhat similar. In Colonial times it was discovered that the *chile* proved a good 'cure' for a hangover, or at least alleviated the symptoms. No doubt the Aztecs were aware of this, but drunkenness was frowned upon in their society.

Basket of *chiles* paid as tribute to the Aztec capital. Codex Mendoza.

Although *chile* is cultivated in many parts of the world, including America, Europe and the Far East, Mexico continues to be the major producer and consumer of *chiles* and the country where the greatest varieties are found. *Chiles* are sold in fresh and dry form. If you wish to visit a real life museum of *chiles*, spectacular colourful displays can be found in any large market in Mexico. Here you will witness first-hand, mountains of fresh bright red, green and yellow *chiles* and black, red and golden brown dried *chiles* in every conceivable shape and size. If you are confused by all the names, it helps to remember that a fresh *chile* pepper has a different name when dried. *Ancho chile*, for example, is a dried *poblano chile*, and *chipotle chile* is a smoked, dried *jalapeño chile*. We have listed some common fresh *chiles* with their equivalent name when dried. For suppliers of fresh and dry *chiles* in the United Kingdom see the list at the end of this book.

Fresh Chile	Dry Chile
Poblano	Ancho, Mulato (*poblano* dried)
Chilaca	Pasilla (*chilaca* dried)
Jalapeño	Chipotle (*jalapeño* smoked and dried)
Mirasol	Guajillo

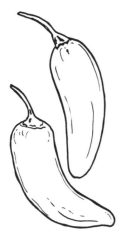

Ancho chile.

Chiles in Mexico are used fresh, dried, sliced, chopped, pureed, cooked and uncooked. They are used for the *salsas* or sauces that accompany all the popular Mexican delicacies (such as *tacos*, *quesadillas* and *tostadas*). *Chile* sauces are generally served in bowls separate to the appetizer on offer, so that each person can season according to individual preference. This is very useful for foreigners travelling in Mexico, who do not like hot food. You will often find a dish of the mild pickled *jalapeño chiles*, sliced or whole in vinegar, close at hand anywhere where food is served. Most Mexicans feel their food lacks an essential ingredient if these *salsas* and *chiles* are not available, but this does not mean that all Mexicans like hot food.

Chiles are used to season dishes, or as the basis of the dish itself. They are essential ingredients in *moles* and *enchiladas* and the strength will vary. If you are in any doubt at a restaurant just ask if the dish is hot (*¿Pica?*). *Chiles* are also served whole. Large fresh *poblano chiles* are stuffed and usually coated in a delicious batter to make *chiles rellenos*. As these *chiles* are not widely available in the United Kingdom (except by mail order) I tend to eat nothing else for the first few days on any trip to Mexico. *Poblano chiles* are also used to prepare *chiles en nogada* a famous dish of stuffed *poblanos* served with a walnut sauce and a sprinkling of pomegranate kernels. The green, white and red colours are the patriotic colours of the Mexican flag. The dish is popular in September, the month of the anniversary of Mexican Independence, when fresh walnuts are in season. *Chile* powder is rarely added to dishes in Mexico, like it is in the United Kingdom. It is generally used on fresh fruit (such as mangoes and oranges), or vegetables, like cucumber and corn on the cob.

Jalapeño chiles.

The flavour of the *chile* is contained in the outer flesh. The 'heat' or piquant quality is derived from *capsaicin* contained in the placenta and veins of the *chile* pod. *Capsaicin* is also distributed unevenly in the flesh. It has no flavour, smell or taste, but rouses the pain receptors of the mouth, causing a burning sensation. The pleasure endorphins released by the brain in response to this 'burn' explain the attraction. The more an individual consumes *chile*, the more desensitized the receptors become, thus creating 'addiction' and tolerance for hotter varieties. Contrary to popular belief, the seeds contain no capsaicin. The seeds are often 'hot' because they come into contact with the placenta during harvest, in transit or through handling. Generally the smaller the *chile* is the hotter it is, because the concentration of seeds is greater.

The placenta of the *chile* pepper contains the most capsaicin, a chemical which causes a burning sensation in the mouth.

The 'heat' in different varieties of *chile* is measured in *Scoville units* or parts per million of capsaicin. *Habanero chiles* were once considered the hottest, measuring up to 300,000 units, but Far Eastern varieties have now taken over. Indian scientists purport that their Tezpur *chile* measures 855,000 units, which if true, makes it the hottest *chile* in the world. By far the majority of *chiles* consumed fall way at the other end of the scale, but as usual it is the showstoppers that hit the headlines. Bell peppers and sweet peppers contain no capsaicin. *Poblano chiles* contain 1000-1500 units and *jalapeños* 2000-2500, not amounts to be afraid of. If in doubt, just try a little at first. You can reduce the heat by removing the seeds and veins during preparation. Always use disposable vinyl gloves when preparing *chiles* or your hands will suffer the consequences.

The cultural and religious significance of *chile* in many parts of Mexico today, particularly in indigenous communities, is reflected in a host of rituals and popular traditions, many of which have endured since pre-Hispanic times. *Chile* has long been associated with purification and protection against malevolent spirits. In popular culture amulets of *pasilla* and *ancho chile* serve to safeguard the household.

Spirit of the *chile* pepper, paper cut. San Pablito, Puebla. By Benito Zósimo.

In the village of San Pablito, Puebla, one of the many spirits venerated by the Otomí people is the spirit of the *chile*. *Amate paper* cuts in the form of this spirit are made by local people and taken by the shaman to a nearby cave. Here the spirit is consecrated. The paper figures are taken to the fields where they are placed on a small altar with offerings. A dance is performed in honour of the spirit, until midnight when ritual purification takes place. The next day farmers take their figures home, where they are placed on an altar beside a votive candle. Thus the *chile* harvest is protected.

In the small town of Olinalá in Guerrero, which I visited for the first time with group of anthropologist friends, beautiful lacquered crafts are made by hand. Here in October, the *fiesta* of the *chile*, or *masúchiles* is celebrated in honour of St. Francis, the patron-saint of the town. Although the festival is Christian, it retains many characteristics of the pre-Hispanic festival of Ochpaniztli, when it was customary to adorn images of the gods with garlands of *chiles* and *cempasúchil* or marigold flowers. Today large vibrant offerings are constructed in honour of St Francis and are beautifully decorated with orange *cempasúchil* and bright red

and green *poblano chiles*. These offerings are carried with great reverence to the church, where a vigil is kept throughout the night. The next day, the *chiles* are distributed at mass amongst the congregation. The sacred seeds are taken home and treasured, and after several months are planted, safeguarded by St. Francis.

Today *chiles* are grown all over Mexico. Every state has its own particular varieties, which are generally consumed locally. The most popular, *serrano, jalapeño* and *poblano,* are consumed nationally. Most cultivated *chiles* are destined for central markets in Mexico City, Guadalajara and Monterrey, where they are distributed. About a fifth of the total national production is processed for sauces or tins, many of which are now available in the United Kingdom.

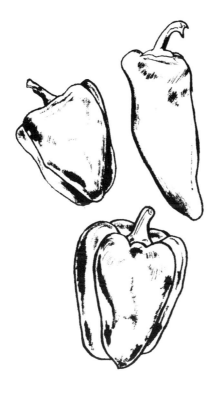

Sweet peppers are *chiles*, but they contain no capsaicin, the chemical responsible for the 'burn' in other pungent varieties.

Preparing fresh *chiles*

In Mexico people use a *comal* or heavy griddle for toasting *chiles*, but if you do not have one, any old frying pan will do. Bell and sweet peppers, which are from the same botanical family, can also be toasted in this way.

Toast the *chiles* or peppers on a hot dry *comal*, griddle or pan (do not use fat and make sure the *comal* is free of grease). Keep turning the peppers over as the skin browns. You can use your fingers at first, but I use tongs, as the peppers get hotter. When the skin begins to blister, place the peppers in a plastic bag and leave them there to sweat for 30 minutes to 1 hour, or until they are cool enough to handle. Do not be tempted to open the bag sooner, as the steam could burn you.

When cool, open the bag and peel the skins off the *chiles*, removing the stalks and seeds. Again remember to wear vinyl gloves to do this job as *chiles* can be very hot. Although you may not feel it at first, you could experience a painful burning sensation on your skin if you do not use protection – you have been warned! The 'burn' will not harm your skin, but it will be very uncomfortable.

Many years ago, when I thought I knew better, I prepared two kilos of *jalapeño chiles*, without using gloves. My hands were so painful, even though I tried all the remedies I had been told about and read in books, such as soaking them in milk. Nothing I did took the pain away, so in the end I went to bed with a bucket of cold water beside my bed, both my hands immersed. When I woke up in the morning, my hands were in perfect condition, with no sign of the previous night's tribulations.

I find toasted *jalapeño chiles* taste so much better for cooking than raw ones. To save time and ensure there is always a supply, I toast batches of two kilos of *jalapeño chiles*. Ordering a box is more cost effective, and once prepared and cleaned, I place them neatly in a tray in the freezer to open freeze them. Once frozen I put the *chiles* loose into a plastic freezer bag and take them out one by one as I need them for cooking.

During the summer months peppers in all colours and varieties are very cheap, so I order one or two boxes from the green grocer and toast them in the same way as *jalapeño chiles*. The smell is wonderful and the taste is heaven, but the best thing is that you have the joy of using them for a few months without having to do the work.

The other advantage of preparing the *chiles* and peppers in bulk is that the smell attracts other members of the family to the kitchen so you do not feel you are left there on your own. They might even volunteer to do some of the work!

For suppliers of fresh and dry *chiles* in the United Kingdom see the list at end of this book.

Chiles poblanos con queso y crema
Poblano chiles with cheese and cream

This recipe makes a wonderful dip for *botanas*.

Ingredients:
1 tin sliced *poblano chiles*
1 small onion finely chopped
1 clove garlic crushed
Grated cheddar cheese
Crème frâiche
Corn or vegetable oil for frying
Salt and pepper to taste

Preparation:
Heat a little oil in a frying pan and fry the onion and garlic until soft and transparent. Add the sliced *poblano chiles* and cook for a couple of minutes. Spoon in enough cream to blend with the *chiles* and add the cheese. Heat until the cheese melts, adding more cream if necessary. Serve as a dip, or *taco* filling.

Chiles jalapeños en vinagre
Pickled jalapeño chiles

One of the things I found hardest to adapt to when I first came to Europe was the absence of pickled *chiles* on the dinner table. They weren't available in any supermarkets. Chipolata sausages (then the King of English sausage), just did not taste right to me without *jalapeño chiles* on the side. When I went to Mexico to show off my five month old daughter Anna, I brought back enough tins of *chiles* to keep me going for a long time, all packed inside her carry cot. In those days, most airlines did not weigh this item of luggage. It would have been simpler to learn how to pickle *chiles*, but I could not buy fresh *jalapeño chiles* then, so I had no choice. Nowadays we are fortunate that we can buy almost anything in our shops and supermarkets, and travel has brought global cuisine closer to every one.

I was first shown how to pickle *chiles* in Oaxaca by my friend Lupita's head cook at her restaurant. I have experimented myself with various recipes over the years, and the results have usually been simple but tasty. In Oaxaca a batch was made every few days, but I have made larger quantities and packed them in glass jam jars. This has given me a supply that lasts for weeks. Friends are always happy to receive them as a gift, just as you would give someone a jar of homemade marmalade or jam.

Ingredients:
1 box (2 kilos) *jalapeño chiles*
1 kilo carrots
2 ½ litres white vinegar
750 ml water
2 onions chopped into small pieces.
Garlic cloves
Herbs and peppercorns
1 teaspoon sugar
1 cube *Knorr* vegetable or chicken stock (optional)
Olive oil for frying

This quantity makes enough to fill 14 or 15 jam jars.

If you prefer to make a smaller quantity just to try or for keeping in the fridge the proportions of vinegar to water are as follows:

750 ml of vinegar
330 ml of water

Preparation:
Always use vinyl gloves when handing *chiles*, especially if you are using large quantities. Prepare the jars by washing them well and warming them in the oven for a while. Wash the *chiles* thoroughly, then remove the stalk and cut the *chiles* lengthways into two or three strips (these are called *rajas* in Mexico). Leave the seeds in the *chiles*. Next peel the carrots, then slice or dice them. They are usually sliced in rings. Peel the garlic cloves and use them whole.

Heat some olive oil in a large pan, preferably a wide shallow one, and when hot add the onions, garlic, *jalapeño chiles* and carrots. Fry for a few minutes, turning the vegetables frequently. Add the peppercorns and herbs. Finally pour in the vinegar and water, bring to the boil and simmer for 3 minutes. When cool, the *chiles* are ready to be bottled.

Jalapeño chiles.

Chiles jalapeños relleños de queso
Jalapeño chiles stuffed with cheese

I learnt this method of preparing *chiles* from my friend Lupita. The *chiles* are steamed while cooking rice. About half way through the cooking of the rice, the *chiles* are placed on top and cooked in the steam. This adds flavour to the rice. You could also steam the *chiles* in a steamer.

Ingredients:
Fresh *jalapeño chiles* (choose nice big round ones)
Fetta cheese
Corn or vegetable oil for frying

For the rice:
1 mug long grain rice
2 mugs boiling water with chicken or vegetable stock cubes or stock
A little oil for frying

To cook rice you need a saucepan with a lid. The proportions are always two mugs of hot water for every mug of rice and one teaspoon of stock granules.

Preparing the *chiles:*
Wash the *chiles* and dry them with kitchen paper. Make a small cut in each *chile* lengthways with a sharp knife. Heat some oil in a small deep frying pan. When hot, deep-fry the *chiles* for a minute or so until the skin looks whitish. Remove the *chiles* from the oil and place in a bowl of cold water. Using vinyl gloves scrape the skin off the *chiles*. Remove the seeds from the inside but leave the stalk. Take care not to break the *chiles*. The flesh should be as firm as it was before you fried them. Stuff the *chiles* with cheese and set aside.

Preparing the rice:

Heat some oil in a saucepan with a lid. Add the rice and fry for a few minutes, stirring continuously, taking care not to burn the rice. Pour the chicken stock slowly and carefully into the rice, as the water will create a sudden rush of steam when it comes in contact with the hot, fried rice. Stir the rice

with the liquid and lower the heat. Place the lid on the saucepan and leave to simmer for 20 minutes. 10 minutes into the cooking of the rice, carefully place the stuffed *jalapeño chiles* on top of the half cooked rice and place the lid back on the pan. Cook for another 10 minutes without disturbing the rice. Then turn off the heat and leave to rest until needed, without disturbing.

Chileajo

On a hot summer's day we do not always feel like preparing a complicated meal. *Botanas* (appetizers) like *chileajo* are a perfect alternative. They are refreshing and light on the stomach. Cold cooked vegetables can be prepared the day before and put together in a few minutes while friends and family are around.

Ingredients:
300 grams potatoes boiled in their skin, peeled and diced
100 grams carrots cooked and diced
100 grams green beans cooked
100 grams peas cooked
1 garlic clove peeled
1 teaspoon oregano
2 *guajillo chiles* (dried *chiles*)
1 cup vinegar (240 ml)
Salt to taste

For garnish:
Feta cheese or *Wensleydale* cheese crumbled
1 small onion sliced in rings
Oregano to taste

Preparation:
Boil the vegetables separately (as different vegetables require different cooking times). Remember to add the greens to the water when it is boiling as this preserves their colour and flavour. Set aside to cool. Potatoes should be boiled in their skin to preserve their goodness, then peeled and diced.
Wash the dried *chiles* well and remove the seeds, veins and stalks. Soak in boiling water (just enough to cover) for about

30 minutes. Puree the *chiles*, garlic, oregano and vinegar and add salt to taste. Once pureed, sieve the mixture.

Mix all the vegetables in a bowl. Pour over the sauce, toss well and garnish with the onion, oregano and cheese.

Cook's tip: For those who dislike raw onion, here is a tip I learnt on one of my trips in Mexico. It improves the flavour significantly and takes the edge off them. Slice the onion finely in rings and place in a dish. Pour enough boiling water to cover them. Leave for a few minutes then drain away the water. Squeeze the juice of one lime over the onion rings. Add to salad or use as a garnish. Serve with *tortilla* chips or fresh bread.

Atun para botanas
Tuna paste for appetizers

Ingredients:
1 small tin tuna
4 tinned *adobado chipotle chiles*
125 grams crème frâiche
100 grams almonds blanched and ground

Preparation:
Puree all the ingredients in a blender and add salt to taste. Keep in the fridge until needed. Serve with *tortilla* chips, salty biscuits, toasted bread or fresh French bread.

Ceramic fish vase
from Tlatilco
800-400 BC.

Caldo Tlalpeño
Tlalpan soup

This soup, from Tlalpan in the south of Mexico City, is my favourite soup when I am travelling in Mexico. It is one of those dishes where the correct ingredients must be used to achieve the right flavour. **Adobado chipotle chile** is the essential ingredient.

Ingredients:
500 grams chicken pieces (thighs and drumsticks are perfect for this soup)
2 carrots pealed and diced
2 small courgettes, ends removed and diced
1 small onion chopped
2 garlic cloves crushed
1 large avocado
1 tomato blanched and chopped
1 or 2 tinned *adobado chipotle chiles*
2 litres stock
Coriander
Salt to taste
Corn or vegetable oil for frying

Preparation:
Boil the stock or water in a large saucepan. Add the chicken pieces and simmer for about 20 minutes until tender. Transfer the chicken to a dish and when cool enough to handle, remove the skin and bones and break the chicken into pieces. Cover and set aside.

Heat the oil in a frying pan and fry the garlic and onion for about 3 to 4 minutes until the onion is transparent. Add the chopped tomatoes and cook for 4 or 5 minutes more. Add this mixture, the *chipotle chile* and the vegetables to the saucepan of soup. Cook until the vegetables are tender. Return the chicken to the saucepan and boil for a few minutes to fully heat the chicken. Serve hot and garnish with strips of avocado.

Salsa de chiles poblanos
Poblano chile sauce

Ingredients:
10 *poblano chiles* (or use 10 green peppers and 3 *jalapeño chiles*)
1 onion chopped
2 or 3 garlic cloves crushed or chopped
250 grams crème frâiche
Salt and pepper to taste
Corn or vegetable oil for frying

Always use vinyl gloves when handling *chiles*, as you will not be aware of their strength until too late. The same type of *chile* can be of a different strength, depending on the harvest.

Preparation:
Toast the *chiles* or peppers on a griddle or frying pan, turning them to toast all sides. Then place the *chiles* in a plastic bag to sweat for about half an hour. When cool enough to handle remove the skin, stalk and seeds. Meanwhile fry the onion and garlic in a frying pan until translucent. Puree the *chiles* with the onion and garlic in a blender. Pour the mixture back into the frying pan and fry for a few minutes. Finally add the crème frâiche and mix well.
Serve with chicken or fish.

Pollo de plaza
Plaza style chicken from Patzcuaro

This is a chicken dish cooked and served on the plaza or main square in Pátzcuaro, Michoacán. If I am travelling on my own in Pátzcuaro, I like to go and eat at the stalls in the plaza. Sitting on the benches, chatting to people, is a good way to find out about all that's happening in the community and feel a part of it. I once sat next to a farmer who was on his way to a Mexico City market to deliver a lorry load of avocados. He was from Uruapan, an hour away from Pátzcuaro, where avocados grow well in the semi tropical climate. I asked him why he had stopped so close from where he had set off. He replied that the *pollo de plaza* in Pátzcuaro was something he always looked forward to when he had to make his six-hour journey to Mexico City to deliver his avocados.

  Pollo de plaza is chicken served on a bed of lettuce, fried with potatoes, carrots and an *enchilada (tortilla)* in a light dried *chile* sauce. It is this sauce that gives the chicken and vegetables their flavour. The dish can be very simple to make if some of the preparations are done in advance, or if you have a supply of dried *chile* sauce in the fridge, perfect for finishing off and serving in the garden.

Ingredients for the chicken (for about 4 people):
1 whole chicken or 8 chicken pieces of your choice
1 onion
2 garlic cloves
Water for boiling
Peppercorns
Bay leaves
Salt

Preparation:
Place all the ingredients in a large saucepan and boil until tender (about 40 to 45 minutes for whole chickens and 20 to 30 minutes for chicken pieces). When cooked set the chicken aside.

For the vegetables:
500 grams potatoes
500 grams carrots

Preparation:
Boil the potatoes with their skin. Then drain and leave to cool before peeling them (run under cold water to speed the process). When cool, peel the potatoes and dice them. Peel the carrots, cut them into strips and boil until tender. Drain and set aside for frying later.

For the dried *chile* sauce:
4 *ancho chiles* (dried *chiles*)
2 garlic cloves
1 small onion roughly cut
I have tried making this dish with tinned *adobado chipotle chile* pureed with a few fresh tomatoes. Sun dried tomatoes may also taste good.

Preparation:
Remove the stalks from the dried *chiles*, then open them up and wash and dry them. Lightly fry the *chiles*, place them in a bowl and pour boiling water over them. Leave for 15 minutes and when cool enough, puree the *chiles* in a blender together with the onion, garlic and a little of the water in which they were soaked. Set aside.

For the enchiladas:
8 *tortillas*
150 grams *Feta* cheese or *Wensleydale* cheese crumbled
4 large lettuce leaves preferably Cox lettuces
Onion finely sliced
Corn or vegetable oil for frying

Preparation:

Heat some oil in a large frying pan. When hot, dip the *tortilla* into the *chile* sauce and fry on both sides quickly. Fold and place on a dish. Repeat with all the *tortillas*. Using the same pan, adding a little more oil if needed, fry the chicken pieces on both sides, then add the potatoes, carrots and more *chile* sauce if necessary.

To serve, spread a lettuce leaf on each plate, and place the chicken on top of the lettuce. Serve the potatoes and carrots alongside, together with the *enchilada*. Sprinkle the crumbled cheese over the *enchilada* and slices of onion. Season with salt.

Cazuela or casserole dish with rich *mole* sauce (pronounced mo-le).

Mole and Pumpkin Seed Sauces

Salsas de Mole y Pepian (Pipian)

Mole (pronounced *mo-le*) is one of Mexico's most famous and traditional dishes, yet until recently was rarely to be found on the menus of Mexican restaurants around the world. This may be because the dish has little in common with the Tex-Mex cuisine that has been heavily promoted by American companies. *Mole* is a rich, luxurious tasting sauce. It takes time to prepare, but to do so is to share in a tradition that dates back hundreds of years. To taste *mole* is to journey deep into Mexico's past and experience a culinary marriage of ancient Mexican and Spanish ingredients.

Mole was a dish that evolved in pre-Hispanic times; its name is derived from the Nahuatl *molli* or *mulli* meaning sauce. *Molli* was essentially a thick sauce made with *chiles*, red tomatoes, ground pumpkin seeds, maize dough and other ingredients, cooked and served with turkey and the meat of other birds and animals known in the pre-Hispanic world.

Many varieties of *mole* existed in ancient Mexico, the potential being limitless given the numerous ingredients available in the market place and the creative methods employed in their elaboration. The Spanish chronicler Sahagún describes different kinds of Aztec *moles* or sauces. One, he said they made with yellow *chiles*; another, *chilmolli*, they made with yellow *chiles* and tomatoes. A simple *mole* of *chile* and red tomato would be added to everyday meat and vegetable dishes. Many ancient varieties are still well known today, such as *mole manchamanteles*, with its characteristically humorous name meaning *the table cloth staining mole!* The famous *mole pepian* gets its name from the *pepitas de calabaza* or pumpkin seeds used as a principal ingredient.

Today the states of Puebla and Oaxaca are the most famous for their *moles*. Oaxaca is known as *the place of the seven moles: negro, coloradito, verde, rojo, manchamanteles, amarillo, and chichilo. Mole poblano*, from Puebla, is probably the most famous of all *moles* today. This is a *mestizo* dish, which originated in seventeenth century Colonial Mexico. Legend has it that a nun at the Santa Rosas convent in Puebla, Maria del Perpetuo Socorro, invented this sumptuous dish. Eager to impress a visiting bishop, Manuel Fernandez de Santa Cruz, who had granted the convent many favours, she put all her culinary expertise to the test. Her efforts were evidently rewarded. Very much impressed, the bishop ordered the monumental *Cocina de Azulejos* or *Tile Kitchen* to be built. This can still be admired today at the ancient monastery and has been converted into a Museum of Ceramics.

Ancient ceramic pot with turkey handle. Tula, Hidalgo 900-1250 AD.

In the strict sense *moles* are sauces prepared with *chiles. Mole poblano*, considered by many to be the national dish of Mexico, is prepared in many different ways. There are about 50 recipes for the dish. I have made my own recipe and often make alterations to it, depending on my mood and the ingredients I have at hand at the time. Although the original recipe was created in a convent in Puebla, today every convent in the town has a different recipe. A *mole fair* is held annually where you can taste and buy an enormous variety of *moles*, in powder form, ready to make.

The *moles* from Puebla are water based and preserved in a dry form, so all you have to do is add chicken stock to convert them back into a sauce. The *moles* from Oaxaca, on the other hand, are fat based so are sold in markets as a paste or cut into a block like cheese.

Pepianes and *mole verde* are true pre-Columbian dishes. As I understand it, *mole verde* is made with *tomatillos*, green herbs and green *chiles*, and *pepianes* are made with pumpkin seeds, sesame seeds, almonds and green *chiles*. Green herbs are not added.

Preparing ingredients for *mole* and *pepian* (pumpkin seed) sauces

Moles and *pepianes* are labour intensive dishes if you are going to prepare them as they were in the villages before modern equipment came to our aid. In Mexico you can buy both *moles* and *pepianes* ready made in a variety of forms, as a liquid in jars and in dried powdered form. Some of the jar presentations are now available in the United Kingdom and are very good. By adding just a few extra ingredients you can make them taste homemade.

When I first wanted to have a go at cooking *mole* many years ago, I had to research how it was prepared in remote villages in Mexico and have a go there myself. I brought back with me a selection of dried *chiles*. The rest of the ingredients were available in the United Kingdom. Having successfully made a go of *mole* I ran out of *chiles* and anybody coming back to Britain from Mexico or California would bring me a kilo of dried *chiles* for my *moles*.

Dried *chiles* are now available in the United Kingdom. They are expensive but I am sure that if people get into the habit of using them and exploit their full potential, demand will grow and prices will come down.

The dried *chiles*

Always use vinyl gloves when handling *chiles* and never touch your eyes with your hands after handling them.

Remove the stalk and set aside the seeds (you may want to add them to a dish later). Remember that the hottest parts of the *chile* are the veins and the seeds in contact with them.

Clean the *chiles*. If you wash them do so quickly under running water and dry them with kitchen paper.

Lightly toast or fry the *chiles* in a little oil, and place them in a bowl. Then pour boiling water over them and leave them to rest for 30 minutes. Puree the mixture in a blender with the liquid. Conventional blenders do not puree the skin of the *chiles* finely so I normally mash the mixture through a wire sieve and discard the pulp.

You can use the *chile* mixture for many other dishes. Use the following method to preserve the it: Heat some oil in a large pan. Add the *chile* mixture and cook for 15 minutes. You can also add pureed garlic and onions.

This mixture can be frozen in small plastic containers, or you can keep it in the fridge in a glass jam jar or pot. It keeps for some time. In fact I have never been able to test how long it keeps as it gets used up so soon! Set the mixture aside while you prepare the rest of the ingredients for the *mole* or *pepian*.

Right: Cholulteca
turkey pot.

Other dry ingredients:
Pumpkin seeds, sesame seeds and almonds

Pumpkin seeds
Use a large shallow pan to toast the seeds, preferably one with a lid as the pumpkin seeds jump all over the place!
Place a handful of pumpkin seeds in a shallow pan and shake them to even the toasting. When they start to jump they are ready. Take care not to burn or brown the seeds as this gives a bitter flavour to the sauce. Remove and repeat until all the seeds are done. With practice you will learn how many to put into the pan in one go. It is useful to prepare more seeds than you need as they are used for many things. I keep mine in an airtight glass jar.

Sesame seeds
Toast the sesame seeds in the same way. I find I can fit more in the pan (compared to the pumpkin seeds) as they do not jump. Toast the sesame seeds evenly taking care not to burn them. They too can be kept in a glass jar for use when needed.

Almonds
Blanch the almonds by placing them in a bowl and pouring boiling water over them. Leave the water to cool until you can put your fingers into the bowl without burning yourself. Remove the skin of the almonds, dry them with a kitchen towel to absorb the moisture and then toast them.
Almonds are easy to toast so I sometimes place a tray in the oven, giving me the chance to finish off other jobs, but you can also toast them in a shallow pan like the other seeds.
        To grind the pumpkin seeds, sesame seeds and almonds I find a coffee grinder is best as you get a very fine mixture that is ideal for making sauces (*moles* and *pepians*).

Fresh chiles
For instructions on how to handle and prepare fresh *chiles*, see the previous chapter: *Chilli*.

Mole poblano
Mole poblano sauce

Ingredients for the *mole* sauce:
300 grams sesame seeds toasted
500 grams almonds toasted
100 grams pumpkin seeds toasted
250 grams sultanas or prunes
3 litres chicken stock or as much as needed
500 grams tomatoes blanched
1 tin *adobado chipotle chiles*
150 grams *ancho chile*
150 grams *pasilla chile*
150 grams *guajillo chile*
2 onions or 200 grams
1 cinnamon stick (ground)
1 teaspoon black pepper corns
1 teaspoon cloves
1 teaspoon aniseeds
1 teaspoon *chile* seeds (optional)
6 tablets Mexican chocolate (such as the *Ibarra* brand)
50 grams French bread
2 or 3 old *tortillas*
Corn or vegetable oil for frying

For the meat:
1 turkey 5-6 kilos (or chicken)
1 onion
1 garlic clove
2 carrots
Bay leaves,
Pepper corns
Salt to taste

How to cook the meat:
Place the turkey or chicken in a very large pan with a lid. Pour in enough water to almost cover the bird, add the carrots, onions, garlic, peppercorns, bay leaves and salt.
Bring to the boil and simmer for an hour or more until tender (depending on the size of the bird).

Leave to cool in the saucepan. When cool enough to handle, cut the turkey (or chicken) in individual portions.

How to make the *mole* sauce:
Prepare the dried *chiles* and nuts as described at the beginning of this chapter.

Heat some oil in a large frying pan, and fry the garlic and onions until soft and transparent. Then add the French bread, *tortillas*, peppercorns, cloves, aniseed and *chile* seeds, followed by the chopped tomatoes and the tin of *chipotle chiles*. Cook for about 10 minutes and when cool enough puree in a blender as finely as you can.

Heat some vegetable oil in a very large, preferably shallow pan. Add the ground seeds and nuts, *chile*, tomato mixture and chocolate with some turkey stock. Simmer, stirring the *mole* continuously to prevent it from sticking to the pan. Cook until a red oily slick appears on the surface (if you are planning to freeze the *mole*, leave it to cool and then store in labelled plastic containers). Add the turkey or chicken pieces to the *mole* and cook for another 15 minutes.

To serve, arrange a piece of turkey on each plate and spoon some *mole* sauce over it. Sprinkle with toasted sesame seeds and serve with rice. A bowl of fresh *salsa* on the table usually complements the cooked ingredients well.

About thirty years ago at a rather formal cocktail party, the conversation turned to Mexican food. One of the guests, who knew I was Mexican, told me that she had been at a Mexican party in the United States. One of the dishes she described was, 'chicken with a revolting chocolate sauce'. I asked her if she had tasted it, presuming she had. Her reply was 'Of course not, how can you have a chocolate sauce with chicken?' She was rather an overpowering person, and my English was not so eloquent in those days so I decided not to enlighten her. *Mole* is not a chocolate sauce: it is a sauce that contains a rich variety of ingredients including dried *chiles*, fruit, nuts, spices and a small amount of bitter natural chocolate. Of course I might have replied that throughout most of its history, cocoa was consumed as a spicy beverage and a bitter ingredient in sauces!

Illustration of a turkey from a Classic Maya painted ceramic vessel.

Turkey

For many of us in Britain, Christmas just would not be the same without Christmas turkey, but few people realise that before the sixteenth century, there was not a single turkey to be found on this side of the Atlantic. Turkeys were named so as it was assumed the exotic bird came from Turkey, but it was in fact introduced to Europe from Mexico.

The people of ancient Mexico were accustomed to a diet based mainly on vegetable products, complemented with products of animal origin obtained on hunting expeditions and through species kept domestically.

Of the abundant animal kingdom that existed in pre-Columbian times many species have survived to this day, not only in their place of origin, but also in many other parts of the world. A fine example is the turkey. In the ancient Americas turkey was known by the indigenous name *huexoloti*, from *huey* meaning large and *xoloti*, the name of an ancient mythological figure. The modern day Spanish name is *guajolote*.

In ancient times the turkey was held in esteem for its delicious meat, which was prized by kings and noblemen. When turkey was first introduced to Europe it was considered a dish of the utmost luxury, which only the wealthy and privileged could afford. It was not until the beginning of the twentieth century, when turkey farms appeared, that this once rare bird began to appear in many households. Norfolk was the most notable area for production.

Think of Mexico next time you eat your Christmas turkey. If it were not for the contribution of the ancient American peoples we would have to make do without one of our most prized traditions.

Left: Cholulteca turkey pot.

Almendrado de Oaxaca
Almond sauce from Oaxaca

The State of Oaxaca in the South of Mexico is known as *the place of the seven moles.* There is so much cultural diversity in Oaxaca, for its jagged mountain ranges are home to many different ethnic groups. Each group speaks its own language and preserves traditions that date back centuries. The *Guelagetza* festival in July attracts hundreds of performers from across the state. Dancers appear dressed in magnificent traditional costume and some carry examples of the crops that are grown in their village of origin. Oaxaca is blessed with an abundance of fresh produce, tropical fruit and fish from its coastline. Each ethnic group has interpreted local ingredients differently to produce one of the most varied cuisines of any state in Mexico.

I took my son Alexander to Mexico when he was 13. Up until then he had been so fussy with his food. During those three weeks in Mexico (a mixture of business and pleasure) he asked for *carne asada con papas fritas* (grilled steak with chips) everywhere we went. When we visited Lupita in Oaxaca, I told Alexander that he had to eat whatever the meal of the day was as it would be rude to ask for his usual dish. We sat in the most magnificent setting admiring the garden, feeling like we were in paradise.

The dish of the day was *almendrado*, a well-known *mole* from Oaxaca. I was amazed to see my usually fussy son eat all of it. Then he asked me something I found hard to answer someone of his age, why I had moved to England if the food was so delicious in Mexico and the county so beautiful. My answer was quite simply that I fell in love! Now I feel at home in both countries, but I could happily spend part of the year in Oaxaca. It is a beautiful place that stimulates the spirit and the people there are so friendly.

Ingredients for the sauce:
500 grams tomatoes blanched (about 6 tomatoes)
125 grams almonds blanched
3 *ancho chiles*

2 slices of French bread or maize *tortillas*
2 level tablespoons sugar
1 litre chicken stock
Corn or vegetable oil for frying

For the meat:
6 pieces of chicken breast or any other pieces you like
2 garlic cloves
1 medium size onion chopped
6 peppercorns
3 cloves
1 cinnamon stick

For garnish:
100 grams almonds blanched and toasted
100 grams green olives stoned and cut in rings

Preparation:
Prepare the dried *ancho chiles* and almonds following the instructions at the beginning of this chapter, then set aside. Boil the chicken in a saucepan with the garlic, onion, peppercorns, cloves and cinnamon stick, for about 20 minutes or until tender. Remove the chicken pieces from the stock. Place the blanched tomatoes, bread and some of the chicken stock (with pepper corns, onion etc.) in a blender and puree to a fine consistency. Set aside.

Meanwhile heat some corn oil in a large shallow pan and fry the pureed dried *chiles* for a few minutes. Add the pureed tomato mixture, bring to the boil and cook for a couple of minutes. Then add the almonds, as much chicken stock as needed and continue to cook, stirring frequently to avoid the mixture burning or sticking to the bottom of the pan. As it boils the sauce will get thicker, so add chicken stock as necessary. Place the ready cooked chicken pieces into the sauce and cook for a few more minutes before serving. Garnish with the olives and almonds. Serve with rice.

As this *mole* sauce freezes very well it is worth making four times the quantity and freezing it in small plastic containers, so all you have to do is boil the chicken and make the rice when you want to use it.

Mole verde

Green mole sauce

Ingredients:

200 grams almonds blanched and toasted
200 grams pumpkin seeds toasted
1 tin green *tomatillos* (200 grams)
1 tin sliced *poblano chiles* (200 grams)
4 *jalapeño chiles*
Chicken stock as required
2 small onions
2 garlic cloves
1 teaspoon of cumin (more if you like it)
1 bunch fresh coriander
Corn or vegetable oil for frying
Salt to taste

Preparation:

Grind the almonds and pumpkin seeds using a coffee grinder or food processor. Blend the *tomatillos*, *poblano* and *jalapeño chiles*, coriander, onion, and garlic with some of the liquid into a fine puree.

Heat some oil in a large pan, add the ground almonds and pumpkin seeds and mix well. Add the pureed ingredients to the pan, mix everything well and add some chicken stock and cumin. Simmer for about 15 minutes taking care that the sauce does not stick to the pan. Add water or stock as needed.

Cook's tip: When cooking with nuts, sauces get thick very easily so add stock until the sauce is the thickness you prefer.

This *mole* can be served with chicken or pork.

Pollo en mole de pistacho

Chicken in pistachio mole sauce

Ingredients:
Chicken pieces for 6 helpings
100 grams pumpkin seeds toasted and ground
100 grams pistachio nuts
50 grams butter
4 tablespoons vegetable oil
Glass of tequila
300 ml chicken stock (more if needed)
250 grams crème fraîche
2 teaspoons cornflour
Salt to taste
A small tin pureed *tomatillos* (optional)

Preparation:
Melt the butter with three spoons of oil in a large pan. Add the chicken and fry on both sides. Pour in the tequila. Bring to the boil and remove from the heat. Then heat a spoon of oil in a separate pan and add the pumpkin seeds. Toss for a couple of minutes, then stir in the chicken stock. Bring to the boil and add the *tomatillos* (if you are using them). Bring to the boil and simmer for 5 minutes. Pour over the chicken pieces and simmer until the chicken is cooked. Stir to prevent the chicken sticking to the pan. Grind ¾ of the pistachios with the crème fraîche and add to the chicken. When serving, sprinkle the remainder of the nuts, cut in smaller pieces, over the sauce. Serve with rice.

Pepian verde
Pumpkin seed sauce

This sauce can be served with chicken, turkey or fish.

Ingredients:
250 grams pumpkin seeds
250 grams crème frâiche
500 ml chicken stock
Bunch of fresh coriander
2 to 4 *anaheim* or *jalapeño chiles* roasted, or tinned *jalapeños*
125 grams unsalted butter
Salt to taste
Freshly ground pepper

For garnish:
For the chicken, toasted pumpkin seeds
For the fish, red onion finely chopped (immerse the onion in a bowl of boiling water for a few minutes. Add the juice of a lemon and drain for use as a garnish).

Preparation:
Melt about 50 grams of butter (or ¼ of the pack) in a large heavy frying pan over a medium high heat, until bubbling. Add the pumpkin seeds (if your frying pan is not large enough do 2 batches). Cook the seeds over a medium low heat for about 3 minutes, shaking the pan and stirring the seeds until they start to pop. Take care or the seeds can fly all over the place! Do not let them burn or brown as this can give a bitter flavour. Remove any dark seeds.

Grind the seeds and melted butter in a blender. Add half the chicken stock, the *crème frâiche, chiles* and coriander. Blend for a minute, add more chicken stock and continue blending until the consistency is creamy. Season with salt to taste.

Melt the rest of the butter in the large saucepan over a high heat until the foam subsides. Add the sauce and stir well. Bring the sauce to the boil and stir. Reduce the heat and bring to the boil again, stirring continuously for about 3 minutes.

This sauce freezes well, so it is worth cooking in large quantities for the freezer. It can also be kept in the fridge for up to a week. Serve with chicken, turkey or fish. If using fish, I suggest you use fillet.

Como cocinar pollo
How to cook chicken

Chicken prepared in this way can be served with all the *mole* and *pepian* sauces, *pollo de plaza*, and any of your own dishes at home. Because the chicken is boiled, a method used in many hot countries, the meat is very moist and tender. The stock left over makes excellent soup.

Ingredients:
1 whole chicken
½ onion
1 clove garlic
Bay leaves
Peppercorns
Pinch of cumin
Water for boiling

Preparation:
Wash the chicken and place it in a large saucepan. Add all the ingredients, with enough water to cover, and boil until tender, for about 40 to 45 minutes. Check the chicken is cooked by piercing the thigh. If the liquid comes out clear, the chicken is cooked. If pink cook for longer. When cooked leave the chicken to cool in its own stock. After about half an hour, remove the chicken.

The stock makes delicious soups. I remove the bay leaves, but don't strain the stock as the onion and garlic disintegrate and the peppercorns usually sink to the bottom. If you are fussy you can strain the stock. I only remove the fat if the stock has been refrigerated and the fat has solidified.

Caldo de pollo
Chicken consommé

If you are cooking chicken for *mole* or any other dish, save the stock for *caldo de pollo*. What is unique about Mexican chicken consommé is the way it is served with limejuice and garnished with freshly chopped onion and coriander.

Ingredients for chicken stock:
Vegetables sliced or diced
You can add any vegetables you like (two or three) such as carrots, courgettes, *chayote*, broccoli, green beans, cauliflower or whatever is in season.

For garnish:
Onion finely chopped
Coriander finely chopped
Limes cut in segments
Fresh avocado sliced (optional)
Pickled *chiles* (optional)

Preparation:
Boil the vegetables you have chosen in the chicken stock, starting with the carrots and green beans that take longer to cook. Taste the stock for flavour. If necessary, add a chicken stock cube or salt.

All the garnishes should be served in small dishes on the table for people to serve themselves. Serve the soup hot in bowls. Squeeze fresh lime juice over the consommé and sprinkle with chopped onion and coriander

If you want a more substantial consommé or light meal, add some pieces of the cooked chicken. I often make consommé when I see chickens on special offer, because it makes use of the stock and leaves the meat for other dishes. You can also use the carcass of your roast chicken.

Como cocinar arroz
How to cook rice

Rice is an excellent compliment to *mole* and *pepian* sauces and accompanies many meat, fish and vegetable dishes in Mexico. Rice is often served as a *sopa seca* (dry soup) before the main course and makes an excellent side dish of its own. Rice is an Old World import to Mexico, introduced by the Spanish after the Conquest. If you like rice and are used to eating it with Oriental food, you'll be interested to see how it is interpreted in Mexico. It has so much flavour and has a distinctive *Mexican* taste. I use Mexican style rice with all my international cooking. If you have difficulties cooking rice, try the Mexican way, which is easy and fool proof. As well as *arroz blanco* (white rice) you can try adding tomato puree to make *arroz rojo* (red rice) or *poblanos chiles* to make *arroz verde* (green rice).

Ingredients:
1 mug long grain rice
2 mugs chicken or vegetable stock (or boling water with stock cubes)
A little corn or vegetable oil for frying

To cook rice you need a saucepan with a lid. The proportions are always two mugs of hot water for every mug of rice and one teaspoon of chicken or vegetable stock granules.

Preparation:
Heat some oil in a saucepan (with a lid). Add the rice and fry for a few minutes, stirring continuously, taking care not to burn the rice. Pour the chicken stock into the rice, taking care not to burn yourself, as the water will create a sudden rush of steam when it comes in contact with the hot, fried rice. Stir the rice with the liquid and lower the heat. Place the lid on the pan and simmer for 20 minutes. Turn off the heat.

Rice cooked on a low heat with this method should always cook perfectly in 20 minutes, provided you do not stir the rice while it is cooking and always remember to place the lid on the saucepan at this stage.

Arroz rojo

To make red rice:

Puree four tomatoes with stock in a blender to make up the two mugs of liquid. The rice will take on the red colour of the tomatoes.

Arroz verde

To make green rice:

Use toasted green sweet peppers or *poblano chiles* instead of tomatoes and follow the same procedure.

Cook's tip: When cooking rice I always make more than the quantity I need. There are many uses for left over rice and this saves you cooking more the next day.

Recipe ideas for *next day* rice:

Arroz frito con chiles poblanos o salsa fresca

Fried rice with poblano chiles or fresh salsa

Preparation:

Heat some oil in a large frying pan and fry a chopped onion until translucent. Then add some rice, chopped *poblano chiles* or peppers, a tablespoon of crème frâiche and mix together.

Cook's tip: If you have made too much *salsa fresca* for a party and are not sure what to do with it next day, cook it with some rice. Fry the *salsa* in a large frying pan for about 5 minutes, then spoon in the left over rice. Stir well to combine the ingredients. This is a quick very tasty meal. You can add any other left over ingredients you like, such as cooked chicken, cooked vegetables or fish.

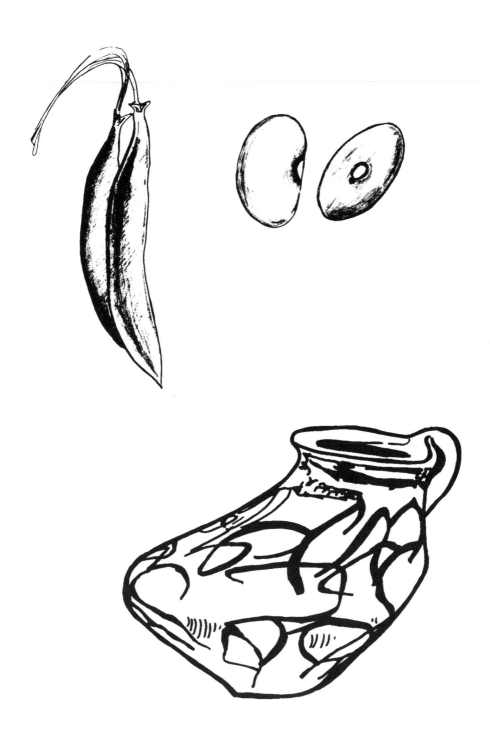

Above: bean pods and seeds.
Below: ceramic *patojo* Mixe bean pot.

Beans

El frijol - Etl - Phaseolus

Ancient beans, discovered by archaeologists inside caves in the high valley of Tehuacan, near Puebla, Mexico, date back six to seven thousand years. Botonists disagree as to when wild beans were first cultivated, but one thing is certain: they have been a staple food for the Mexican people for over two thousand years. Together with maize, squash and *chile*, beans form the basis of Mexican cuisine and are rich in protein and minerals.

There are almost two hundred species of bean, of which four are widely cultivated around the world. The botanical genus is known as *Phaseolus*. With the exception of the broad bean (Vicia faba), staple food of the Romans, and of a different genus, all beans originate in Mexico and the American continent. French and runner beans are still found growing wild in some areas of Mexico, along the roadsides and in the high mountains of the south.

Beans were paid as tribute in ancient Mexico and like cocoa beans, were used as a form of currency. They are depicted in the sixteenth century Codex Mendoza. In his writings about the customs of indigenous peoples in Mexico, the seventeenth century Spanish priest Hernando Ruiz de Alarcón, recalls hearing the chants of farmers in Guerrero as they sowed the seeds of their revered beans.

'*Great spirit clothed in black,*' they sang as they went about their work. The ancient Mexicans utilised many parts of the bean plant for culinary and medicinal purposes: the seeds, pods, flowers and roots were cooked. Dry beans had the advantage of being suitable for storage, and flour was made by toasting and grinding the beans. The Spanish took beans back to Spain with them in the sixteenth century and from there they spread to France, England and beyond. The French word for bean, *haricot*, is derived from one of the *náhuatl*, Aztec words for bean, *ayocotl*.

Below: bean bin depicting tribute paid to the Aztec capital. Codex Mendoza.

The bean features in modern day popular mythology in Mexico. For the Otomi people of the south Huasteca, the bean, like all plants has a soul. A myth relates that because the bean god is black, men did not love or accept him on grounds of his colour. Consequently, man was reproached by this god for his ingratitude.

In another legend, of the Chinantec people of Chinantla, an idol in the form of a cat appears in the village, his presence a guarantee of a good harvest of beans. But when a neighbouring village takes the idol through magic, the harvests are abundant in this place and become scarce in Chinantla.

Spirit of the bean paper cut, San Pablito, Puebla.

Today beans in Mexico are used for cooking in either fresh or dry form and there are many different varieties. Black beans, pinto beans and kidney beans are available in the United Kingdom in health food shops and supermarkets. *Chilli con carne*, which contains kidney beans, is not a Mexican dish: it is a Texan dish. The literal translation from the Spanish (*chile* with meat) means little to the majority of Mexicans.

A humble meal of beans and *tortillas* is within most people's reach in Mexico. I have always maintained that this is much healthier than the fast food alternative, chips or French fries, which many people opt for in Europe and the United States. Beans are packed with protein. When I was a poverty-stricken student, playing host to all my equally impoverished student friends, I often mixed cheese with refried beans and served them on French bread (*molletes*). The result was heaven to hungry souls! No one could quite work out what I had done to the beans. They all assumed I had spent a fortune as their parties usually consisted of drink only. If there was food, it was because they had trapped the pizza man in the lift (if he took more than half an hour to

reach your door, you got the pizza for free!)

The modest bean is well worth considering if you find yourself short of cash and have hungry mouths to feed. Remember though that the bean is an egalitarian pulse and is consumed by all classes of Mexican society. In most Mexican households today it is quite common to have a pot of beans on the go for whenever they are needed. These may last a couple of days to a week and a fresh batch is made regularly.

The so-called 'Mexican Beans' that I have tasted in restaurants in the United Kingdom have usually been quite bland and lack the delicious flavour of beans in Mexico. What you boil them with makes a lot of difference to the flavour. Once cooked, beans can be used in many different ways. They can be made into soups (whole or pureed), or used for refried beans and pasta dishes. Refried beans are generally served as an accompaniment and are wonderful as a dip. They make an indispensable contribution to the breakfast table when they are served at the side of the plate with eggs. Beans complement lunchtime and main meal dishes in the same way. Refried beans are also spread on *tortas* (rolls), *tostadas* (flat fried *tortillas*) and *tacos* along with a host of other fillings and toppings. In this way beans are one of many ingredients (meat, vegetables, cream, avocado, cheese etc.), that contribute to the delicious taste of the whole. *Tortas, tacos* and *tostadas* are enjoyed by all sections of society.

Remember that the perfect combination of ingredients that makes an appetizing bean soup is the result of centuries of experimentation. If you do not want a saucepan of beans resting on your cooker for days, they can be frozen in small containers and taken out for Sunday morning brunch or on a cold winter's day when wholesome comfort food is welcomed.

Como cocinar frijoles
How to cook beans

Ingredients for the beans:
500 grams pinto beans, kidney beans, or black beans
1 medium sized onion cut into quarters
3 garlic cloves
3 bay leaves
2 tablespoons dried *epazote* or coriander
Chicken or vegetable stock

Preparation:
Wash and rinse the beans well. Place them in a large pan and add plenty of water to cover them. The beans will absorb a lot of water and double in size, so make sure you add plenty of water. Leave the beans to soak overnight.

Another method can be used to reduce the soaking time. Place the beans in a large basin and pour boiling water over them. When the beans have absorbed the water, after 30 minutes, add more boiling water to fully cover the beans. They are ready to cook after soaking for 2 to 4 hours.

To cook the beans, place them in a large saucepan with the water used to soak them. Add the onion, garlic, herbs and enough water to cover them well. Cook for approximately 1 ½ hours or until tender.

Important note: never add cold water to the beans while they are being cooked. If more liquid is needed, add only boiling water.

Once cooked, remove the bay leaves. The beans can be used in many different ways, as you need them.

Frijoles de olla
Beans cooked from the pot

These beans are called *frijoles de olla* because they are eaten straight from the pot as they are, without any further preparation. To make them, prepare the beans (see *How to cook beans*), adding a piece of meat for flavouring. This could be a whole *chorizo* sausage or a piece of pork on the bone with plenty of fat. I once bought a whole leg of Spanish *jamon serrano* (smoked ham). Five weeks later when we had devoured the lot, we were left with the bone and fat. All this went into a pot of beans and made the most delicious *frijoles de olla*. You can be creative, especially if you have a friendly butcher.

Frijoles pintos con tocino
Pinto beans with bacon

Ingredients:
500 grams pinto beans
10 rashers streaky bacon rinds removed
2 small onions chopped
4 garlic cloves crushed
1 teaspoon oregano (dried if fresh is not available)
2 tablespoons dried *epazote* or coriander (fresh or dry)
2 or 3 bay leaves
4 tomatoes skinned and chopped
4 *chiles* roasted

Preparation:
Prepare and cook the beans. See *How to cook beans.*

Heat some oil in a large saucepan and fry the crushed garlic, onion and bacon (cut into small pieces). Cook for a few minutes until the onion is soft and transparent, add the chopped *chiles*, tomatoes and herbs. Add the cooked beans and heat thoroughly.

Frijoles refritos
Refried beans

Ingredients:
See *How to cook beans*

To garnish:
Wensleydale cheese

Preparation:
Heat some vegetable oil in a frying pan (you can be generous with the oil). Add 2 to 3 serving spoons of already cooked beans to the pan. Using a potato masher, pulp the beans, adding more for desired quantity. The beans will absorb the oil. Add more oil if needed. Serve with any dish, such as eggs for breakfast or a lunchtime meal. Sprinkle with crumbled *Wensleydale* cheese.

Molletes
Crusty rolls spread with beans and salsa

Ingredients:
French rolls
Refried beans (See *How to cook beans*)
Cheddar cheese finely sliced or grated
Onion finely sliced or chopped
Tomato chopped or *salsa* (any kind)

Preparation:
Cut the rolls lengthways and remove some of the inside: in Mexico people prefer the crispy part. Spread both halves of the bread with refried beans and add the cheese. Place under a hot grill or in a pre-heated oven to allow the cheese to melt. Top with the onion and *salsa*.
Cook's tip: The onion tastes really good if blanched and soaked in lime (this takes away the sharpness). Top with chopped tomato or *salsa*, ideally *salsa fresca*. The combination of refried beans and the fresh ingredients is delicious. Serve and eat immediately.

Sopa de frijol
Bean soup

There are many ways of making this every day Mexican soup. Here I have included my favourite recipe though I am giving ideas for variations. With an understanding of the basics you can make up your own.

Ingredients for the beans:
500 grams pinto beans, kidney beans, or black beans
1 medium sized onion cut into quarters
3 garlic cloves
2 or 3 carrots peeled and diced
3 bay leaves
2 tablespoons dried *epazote* or coriander

For the tomato sauce:
4 tomatoes blanched (skin removed) and chopped
2 garlic cloves crushed
1 medium onion chopped
Pinch of oregano
4 *chiles* toasted with skin removed, or a tin of *jalapeño chiles*

Preparation:
Prepare and cook the beans with the carrots (see *How to cook beans*). Remove the bay leaves, and puree the rest in a blender or food processor, adding more liquid if necessary.

To make the tomato sauce, fry the onion and garlic and when transparent, add the chopped tomatoes and *jalapeño chiles*. Cook for a few minutes and add the fresh herbs if you are using them (or dried herbs such a mixed herbs, oregano, marjoram and parsley). Add the pureed beans to the sauce and bring to boil.

This soup freezes very well. I often make larger quantities and freeze it concentrated in containers. This way you only need to add stock or water and adjust the seasoning when you want to use it.

Sopa de fideo con caldo de frijol
Vermicelli and bean soup

Bean soup, prepared and frozen in small containers (250 grams) makes quick very delicious soup.

Ingredients:
2 nests fine *vermicelli* pasta
Pureed bean soup from your ready-frozen supply (see *How to cook beans*)
Liquid stock as needed
Corn or vegetable oil for frying
Salt to taste

Garnish:
Wensleydale cheese crumbled
Crème frâiche

Preparation:
Heat some oil in a large saucepan and when hot add the *vermicelli* pasta, crushing it in your hand so that it breaks into small pieces. Lightly fry the *vermicelli* until golden brown, taking care not to burn it. Add three cups of water or stock, bring to the boil and simmer for 10 minutes. Add ready prepared pureed bean soup. Boil until the *vermicelli* is tender.

Most pasta soups can be served *aguada* (liquid) *or seca.* (dry/without liquid) If dry, add less stock. When serving *sopa seca* (dry soup) add crème frâiche and sprinkle with crumbled *Wensleydale* cheese.

Sopa de papa
Potato soup

Like bean soup, potato soup is wholesome and comforting when it is home made. Potatoes originated in South America: the past only wild varieties were found in Mexico, but today potatoes are widely cultivated, as they are in many parts of the world.

Ingredients:
500 grams potatoes (3 to 4)
100 grams onion chopped (one small or half large)
2 tomatoes blanched and chopped
1 ½ litres chicken or vegetable stock
2 or 3 garlic gloves crushed or chopped
Herbs fresh or dried (e.g. mixed herbs, parsley)
1 *jalapeño chile* chopped (fresh and toasted or pickled)
Corn or vegetable oil for frying
Salt and pepper to taste

Preparation:
Peel the potatoes and grate or cut them. Heat the vegetable oil in a saucepan and fry the chopped onions and garlic until translucent. Add the chopped tomatoes and *chile,* stir and cook for a couple of minutes. Add the chopped potatoes and cook for a further 2 to 3 minutes. Pour in the chicken stock and add the herbs. If using stock cubes do not add extra salt as they tend to be salty. Cook for about 14 minutes until the potatoes are tender. Season with salt and pepper to taste. Serve hot.

Sopa de poro y papa
Leek and potato soup

Ingredients:
4 or 5 leeks
3 or 4 potatoes
1 onion chopped
2 cloves of garlic crushed
Parsley (fresh or dry)
Chicken or vegetable stock
Milk
Corn or vegetable oil for frying
Salt and pepper to taste

Preparation:
Chop the leeks finely into rings and wash thoroughly, making sure there is no soil between the layers. Then peel the potatoes and cut into small pieces or grate using a large grater.

Fry the garlic and chopped onions in a large saucepan for 2 to 3 minutes. Add the leeks and simmer on a low heat for a few more minutes or until the leeks are slightly translucent. Put in the potatoes, cook for a couple of minutes and add the stock and parsley. Cook for about 30 minutes until tender. Add milk when ready to serve and season to taste.

This soup freezes very well. As leeks are cheap when in season, this is a good time to stock up for the rest of the year. As for all soups, do not freeze with milk. This can be added when serving.

Crema de zanahoria
Carrot soup

I often add pureed carrot soup to clear soups to give them a creamy texture and to just about any other soup to give body and build up quantity. Carrots were introduced to Mexico after the Spanish Conquest; they are used for soup, served with main course dishes, and are chopped and pickled with *chiles*.

This is a carrot soup I have been making for years, which my family love.

Ingredients:
500 grams carrots peeled and chopped
1 potato peeled and chopped
1 onion cut in quarters
2 garlic cloves
6 pepper corns
Pinch of ground nutmeg
4 cloves
Chicken or vegetable stock
Fresh coriander chopped
Milk or water to taste
Salt and pepper to taste
Butter

Preparation:
Boil the carrots, potato, onion and garlic in a large saucepan with the chicken or vegetable stock (enough to cover the vegetables). Add the peppercorns, nutmeg and cloves and cook over a medium heat for about 20 minutes. Leave the soup mixture to cool, then puree in a blender. Melt the butter in a large saucepan and when bubbling add the soup mixture, chopped coriander and bring to the boil. Add the milk or water and taste for seasoning.

If you plan to freeze this soup, freeze the pureed ingredients without milk. Without milk the soup will keep in the freezer for much longer (add milk or water before heating). The choice of milk or water is very much up to personal preference. Milk will make the soup creamier and water make it lighter. This soup is very economical to make when carrots are in season. I make it in large quantities at this time of year and freeze it. It is also very useful for thickening other vegetable soups.

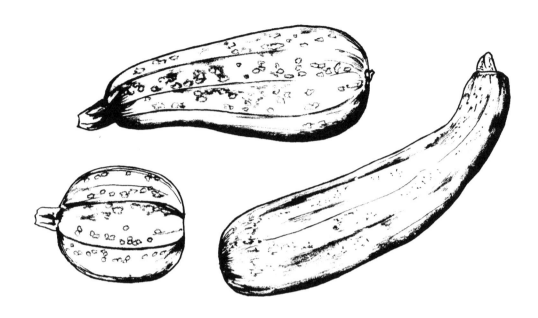

Marrow.

Marrow, Pumpkin and Squash

La calabaza - Ayutli - Cucurbita

The word *calabaza* in Mexico is used to describe the squash family of vegetables (courgette, zucchini, pumpkin, gourd etc.). Squash is a vegetable that has sustained the Mexican people for centuries, together with maize, bean and *chile*. It was highly valued in pre-Hispanic times and this is reflected in the arts where countless references are made to this vegetable: giant gourds were sculpted from stone and ceramic vases were frequently fashioned in the form of squash. Today gourds are an inspiration to potters, copper and silver smiths. Dried gourds are used in many popular arts.

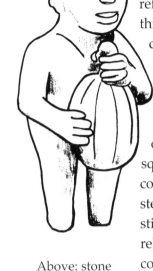

Above: stone sculpture of a man carrying a gourd. Brooklyn Museum, New York.

Right: Late Post Classic stone scupture of a marrow.

In the sixteenth century, Spanish chroniclers observed that when the people of ancient Guerrero planted squash seeds, they spoke to Mother Earth, asking her to cover and protect the seed, lest a tiny ant should covert and steal it from her. Today in indigenous communities there are still many rituals associated with the sowing of seeds. The religion of the Cora Indians of Nayarit, who live in isolated communities of the Sierra Madre, is a mixture of ancient beliefs and Catholicism. In October, the Cora dedicate a festival to maize and squash and perform dances that represent the planting of these crops. Squash and maize are cooked in large pots, hung as an offering to the gods, then shared among the participants of the festival.

Non-edible varieties of gourd have long been cultivated in Mexico for ritual use. Today in the village of Tequesquinahuac, in the Texcoco area, the rainmaker Timoteo Hernandez uses a gourd in a ritual to petition the rains. He burns insence and fills a hollow gourd or *jícara* with holy water and cotton bolls, which represent clouds. Reverently, Timoteo makes the sign of the cross. With palm leaves in his hands, he prays for the dark clouds that will unleash rain on the local fields.

Gourds have many practical uses. In pre-Hispanic Mexico, and in *pulque* producing areas today, gourds are used to siphon maguey juice from the heart of the plant. Once fermented, this juice becomes the *pulque*, the alcoholic beverage. Dried, hollowed gourds are used as containers, for carrying water, *pulque*, and for storing seeds and grains. They are also used for serving food and beverages, notably hot chocolate. For centuries gourds have been used for making musical instruments such as *maracas* or shakers and *guirros* or scrapers. In pre-Hispanic Mexico, dried gourds were even used to carry goods across rivers, by joining them together and using them as floats.

Above: dried, hollow gourd used to carry water or pulque (fermented agave juice). A dry corn cob acts as a stop.

In many parts of Mexico today, beautiful crafts are made from gourds. In the small town of Olinalá in Guerrero, famous for its fine lacquer work, gourds are lacquered and painted. Exquisite gourd lampshades hang in the church of the town. Not far away in the village of Temalacatzingo, armadillos, turtles, other animals and toys are made from gourds.

Whenever I taste the delicacies my mother prepares with courgettes, I come to the conclusion that this family of vegetables has yet to fulfil its potential in Europe. I have often been given marrow by people who grow it. They tell me they have eaten stuffed marrow and marrow stew until it is coming out of their

Below: armadillo from Temalacatzingo, Guerrero. The body is made from a gourd.

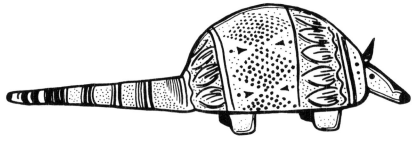

ears and don't know what to do with it! Gardeners seem to get a lot of satisfaction out of growing squash and entering competitions, but could do with some inspiration when it comes to using it creatively in the kitchen. Perhaps because squash is native to Mexico, it is used in such a variety of ways, some of which we would do well to adopt here. In Mexico the flesh of the fruit is used to make savoury soups and dishes as well as sweet *dulce de calabaza*, pie and jam. Courgette flowers are considered a delicacy. The seeds are also toasted and ground to make soups and *pepianes* or sauces.

Sopa de calabacitas y elote
Courgette and sweet corn soup

Ingredients:
4 courgettes grated (uncooked)
2 tomatoes blanched and chopped
1 onion chopped
1 garlic glove crushed or chopped
100 grams tinned or ½ mug frozen sweet corn
1½ litres chicken or vegetable stock (fresh or granules)
Epazote or parsley
Corn or vegetable oil for frying
Salt and pepper to taste

For garnish:
Grated cheese

Preparation:
Fry the onion and garlic until soft and transparent. Add the chopped tomatoes and fry for about 2 minutes. Add the courgettes, sweet corn, herbs and stock. Cook for about 15 minutes until the courgettes are tender and the flavours have blended. Serve hot and garnish with grated cheese.

Sopa de calabacitas con cilantro
Courgette and coriander soup

Ingredients:
12 courgettes cooked (boiled in chicken or vegetable stock)
1 litre chicken or vegetable stock
1 small onion chopped
Bunch of coriander
Butter for frying
Salt and pepper to taste

Preparation:
Puree the pre-cooked courgettes and coriander in a blender, adding stock if necessary. Melt the butter in a saucepan and fry the onion until soft and transparent. Add the pureed courgettes and fry for 5 minutes on a low heat. Add the chicken or vegetable stock and salt to taste. Bring to the boil and turn off the heat. Serve hot.

Crema de calabacitas y pepitas
Courgette and pumpkin seed soup

Ingredients:
8 courgettes or 1 ½ kilos
200 grams pumpkin seeds toasted or fried
1 ½ litres chicken or vegetable stock
Milk to taste
Butter (for frying the pumpkin seeds)
Salt and pepper to taste

Preparing the pumpkin seeds:
There are two ways to prepare the pumpkin seeds. One is to melt some butter in a large saucepan and when hot, add the pumpkins seeds. Stir for an even fry: the seeds are ready when they start to jump. Take care not to burn or brown them as this will give a bitter flavour. Use this *wet* method if you have a blender or food processor to grind the seeds.

The other method it is to toast the seeds and use a coffee or nut grinder to grind the seeds. Toast them for a few minutes, shaking the pan and taking care not to burn them.

Store in an airtight container until needed.

Preparating the courgettes:
Cook the courgettes with the chicken or vegetable stock for about 15 minutes or until tender. When cool puree the courgettes with their liquid (with the pumpkin seeds if using the wet method). Leave some seeds aside for garnish. Pour the mixture into the pan and bring to the boil. Add more stock if needed and the milk. Put the reserved pumpkin seeds in and season with salt and pepper to taste. Serve hot.

When using the toasted method, melt some butter in a pan. Add the toasted ground pumpkin seeds and stir until they absorb the butter. Add the pureed courgettes, more stock if needed, and the milk. Season with salt and pepper.

This soup freezes very well, so it is worth making a larger quantity and freezing (do not add milk). Defrost when needed and just add the milk, extra stock if needed and seasoning before serving. When courgettes are in season during the summer they are very cheap. If you do not feel like cooking them, you can freeze them.

Freezing courgettes to be used for soups later:
Wash the courgettes, trim away the ends and cut or dice. Open freeze on a tray in a deep freezer. When frozen store them in plastic bags loose (this way they take less space). When needed, cook the courgettes from frozen, simmering in boiling water until soft.

Cooking times for the courgettes:
Boiled whole for 7 minutes
Steamed for 15 minutes
Cut in rings and fried for 15 minutes

Cook's tip: The advantage of boiling the courgettes whole is that they retain their crispiness inside. After boiling them, run them under cold water to prevent them from further cooking in their own heat. I sometimes boil the courgettes for less time (5 to 6 minutes) and set aside without pouring cold water over them (if I am to use them shortly).

Calabacitas con queso y crema
Courgettes with cheese and cream

Ingredients for the courgettes:
4 Courgettes
Cheddar cheese or *mozzarella* (as much as you like)
Crème frâiche (to taste)
Salt to taste

Ingredients for the tomato sauce:
4 tomatoes blanched and chopped
1 small onion
1 garlic clove
1 *jalapeño chile* toasted and chopped (or tinned *chile*)
Pinch of dried oregano
Fresh or dried herbs (coriander, parsley etc.)

Preparation:
Follow the instructions *How to make tomato sauce* in the Chapter: *Tomato.*

The courgettes

Wash the courgettes and trim the ends. Boil for 7-8 minutes, drain and run under cold water to stop them cooking further in their own heat. Cut the courgettes in rings, cubes, or lengthways into long pieces. Add the courgettes to the tomato sauce. Add the cheese, cook until the cheese melts and add the crème frâiche. Season with salt and pepper to taste.

You can prepare this dish the day before you need it. Get together all your pre-cooked, chopped ingredients and place in an oven proof dish with the tomato sauce. Add the grated cheese and crème fraiche, cover and place in the fridge until next day. When you are ready to use the dish, remove the cling film and place the dish in a hot oven for 15 minutes, or until the sauce bubbles and the cheese melts.

Calabacitas a la mexicana
Courgettes Mexican style

Ingredients:
½ kilo courgettes par boiled
4 tablespoons cooked sweet corn
Poblano chiles or green peppers toasted and cut in strips
Jalapeño chiles toasted and cut in strips
3 tomatoes toasted and blanched
1 onion chopped
1 or 2 garlic gloves crushed or chopped
Parsley fresh or dried
100 grams mild cheddar cheese grated
Corn or vegetable oil for frying (about 2 tablespoons)
Salt to taste

Preparation:
Fry the onion and garlic in a large frying pan until translucent. Add the tomatoes and fry for 2 minutes. Add the parsley, *chiles* or peppers, sweet corn and courgettes and cook for a couple of minutes for the flavours to blend. Sprinkle with grated cheese and salt to taste. Serve hot.

Calabacitas al mojo de ajo

Courgettes in garlic

Ingredients:

500 grams courgettes (about 4 small ones)
Unsalted butter
5 garlic cloves finely sliced
Juice of 1 lime
¼ teaspoon freshly ground black pepper
Dried oregano
2 tablespoons parsley
Corn or vegetable oil for frying
Salt to taste

Preparation:

Wash and slice the courgettes. Drain in a colander, add salt and set aside for 30 minutes. Meanwhile, heat the oil and butter in a frying pan, add the garlic and stir frequently until golden but not brown. Drain the garlic and set aside. Add the courgettes to the pan and fry for 8 to 10 minutes until browned but still crisp. Add the lime juice and garlic, toss thoroughly and add the black pepper, oregano and parsley. Serve with French bread for a light lunch.

Crepas de flor de calabaza
Crêpes with courgette flowers

Courgette or pumpkin flowers are considered a delicacy in Mexico, where they are sold in colourful piles in the market place. Courgette flowers cannot be purchased fresh in the United Kingdom (unless the idea catches on soon), but you can collect your own if you grow them. Alternatively, make friends with your local farmer if you live in the country, (as I have done). They can now be purchased in tins from the Mexican company *Herdez* under the *Doña Maria* brand name.

Ingredients for the filling:
1 or 2 cooked courgettes diced finely
2 to 4 tomatoes blanched and chopped
1 small onion chopped
Bunch of courgette/pumpkin flowers cooked in boiling water and chopped.
1 *poblano chile* toasted skin removed and chopped
Sweet corn (tinned, fresh or frozen. 1 small tin or half a cup)
Crème frâiche
Grated cheddar cheese

For the crêpes:
100 grams flour
300 ml liquid (half milk/ half water)
1 egg
Pinch of salt
1 tablespoon corn or vegetable oil

Preparation for the filling:
Butter an ovenproof dish, preferably a rectangular or square one and set aside. Heat some oil in a large frying pan and fry the onion until translucent. Add the chopped tomatoes and cook for 2 to 3 minutes. Then add the cooked courgettes, sweet corn, chopped courgette flowers, *chiles* and half the crème frâiche. Heat to allow the flavours to mix and add salt and pepper to taste.

For the crêpe or pancake mixture:

Sift the flour with the salt in a bowl. Make a well in the middle and add the egg. Gradually add the diluted milk, stirring continuously. When half the liquid has been added, stir in the oil and beat the mixture until smooth. Add the remaining milk, mix well and leave to stand for 30 minutes. The batter should have the consistency of thin cream. If too thick, add a little more milk or water. For savoury pancakes I prefer to add water.

How to make the crêpes:

Use a pan the size of the pancakes you want to make (I prefer small ones). Grease the pan lightly (you need very little oil) and heat on a moderate heat. When hot, spoon one table-spoon of batter onto the pan. Tilt immediately so that the batter covers the pan evenly. Cook until the underside of the pancake is golden brown. Turn by running a palette knife under the pancake and turn over. Or toss them if you are feeling more adventurous! Cook the other side for about ten seconds. Repeat until all the pancake mixture is used up.

Fill the pancakes with one or two teaspoons of the courgette flower filling, depending on the size of the pancakes. Roll the pancakes around the filling and place each crêpe in the dish. Spoon on the rest of the crème frâiche and sprinkle the grated cheese over the crêpes. Heat in the oven until the cheese has melted. Serve with green salad and French bread.

These crêpes freeze very well and I usually make all the pancakes, fill them, place them on a tray and open freeze them. When frozen I transfer the crêpes to a plastic bag, label and seal the bag for use when needed.

When you want to use the crêpes, take them out of the freezer and place them on a plate (2 to 3 per person). Heat them in the microwave for two minutes, spoon crème frâiche over them and sprinkle on some grated cheese. Return to the microwave and heat for another minute or two. The the crêpes are now ready to eat. Serve with salad and bread.

I frequently offer this dish as a vegetarian alternative in my restaurant, but it is appreciated by anyone. Other

guests usually look enviously on when the sizzling plate is presented at the table. In Mexico crêpes are very popular and there are restaurants that specialise in them. The variety of fillings is enormous, so you can be creative. Try using some of the *taco* fillings, the sweet corn and *poblano chile* filling, *huitlacoche* or invent your own.

Crêpes and other French delicacies such as breads, pastries and creme caramel were introduced to Mexico in the nineteenth century when the French occupied the country and the Austrian-born emperor Maximilian ruled as emperor.

Pumpkin seeds

Another part of the squash plant that is widely used in Mexico is the seed. For recipes of dishes made with pumpkin seeds, see the chapter: *Mole and Pumpkin Seed Sauces.*

Ancient flat stamp of a flower, from the State of Mexico. Motif by Jorge Enciso.

Tomato

El jitomate - Xitomatl - Lycopersicum esculentum

The tomato, a plant belonging to the genus *Lycopersicon*, is a fruit that needs little in the way of introduction, for it has been embraced enthusiastically around the world. It is hard to imagine Italian food without tomatoes; many pizza toppings, pasta sauces and salads would not exist without them. Tomato ketchup is king in the fast food trade and British baked beans would have no sauce without them. However, the history of the tomato in Europe is relatively recent. Introduced from Mexico in the sixteenth century, many years passed by before the tomato's potential was fully realised.

When the Spanish conquered Mexico in 1521, the tomato was already widely cultivated throughout Central America. Wild tomato plants originated in South America, but genetic and cultural evidence suggest that the plant was first cultivated in Mexico: old European cultivars are genetically similar to tomatoes domesticated in ancient Mexico; there are no representations of tomatoes in South American ceramics and textiles, though it was usual for these cultures to depict the crops that were important to them on; nor is there a word for the plant. This has led some experts to conclude that domestication took place further north.

The Aztecs called the large red variety of tomato *xitomatl,* and the small green variety, which was cultivated with the maize crop, *tomatl* (the English word *tomato* is derived from this *nahuatl* word). They had many uses for the tomato: they made drinks from the juice by pounding the flesh in a *molcajete* with *zapote* (a fruit), a herb called *epazote,* a pepper known as *xoxoxochitl* and a red spice, *achiote.* This concoction was mixed with water and pineapple juice. Long before the Europeans had any inkling of the tomato's existence, the Mexicans were using the fruit to make soups and sauces. They did so with the ingredients known to them;

chile, squash, native onions, maguey syrup and spices. The tomato, rich in vitamins, was also used for its medicinal properties.

The Aztecs taught the Spaniards how to use tomato in cooking, on its own and mixed with peppers. Plants were taken to Spain after the Conquest of Mexico, and spread to Italy in the seventeenth century. It may come as a surprise to many that tomatoes were viewed with some suspicion in Northern Europe at first. This is partly because the plant is similar in appearance to Deadly Nightshade (*Atropus belladonna*): most of the plants of this family known then in Europe were poisonous. Also unappealing was the tomato's acidity when consumed raw as a fruit. Furthermore, it could only be cultivated in a warm climate.

It was not until the nineteenth century that the fruit, commonly considered a vegetable, became a popular ingredient for cooking. Its use in Western countries soared in the early 1920's with the arrival of mass canning and the invention of juice extractors. Soon afterwards the young entrepreneur Joseph Campbell found a willing market for canned tomatoes and went on to establish a company of international acclaim. Thanks to modern cultivars and improved transportation, tomatoes are available almost everywhere throughout the year. They are essential providers of vitamins and minerals.

In Mexico, as in ancient times, tomatoes are consumed raw and cooked, as they are all over the world today. They are essential ingredients in many fresh *salsas* and cooked sauces. Mexican tomatos are rich in flavour because they are ripened in the sun and are harvested later. Most people prefer the large varieties, as they are the juiciest. *Tomatillos,* or *green tomatoes,* as they are known in the United States, are not under ripe tomatoes. In fact they are not tomatoes at all. They belong to the genus *Physalis*, the same family as the gooseberry.

Salsa fresca
Fresh salsa

This is the *salsa* I prepare for all my *botanas* (appetizers), as I just love it. My friend Lupita from Oaxaca, passed her recipe on to me.

Ingredients:
2 small tomatoes blanched and chopped
1 small onion finely chopped
1 *jalapeño chile* seeded and finely chopped
2 teaspoons olive oil
1 teaspoon vinegar
1 teaspoon lime juice
½ teaspoon dried leaf oregano crushed
½ teaspoon salt

Preparation:
Place the tomatoes, onion and *chile* in a medium sized bowl. Add olive oil, vinegar, limejuice, oregano and salt. Mix well. Let the *salsa* stand for 2 hours for the flavour to blend. Serve at room temperature.

Salsa pico de gallo
Pico de gallo fresh salsa

This is a very common *salsa* found in many parts of Mexico. What it is called depends on where you are, but basically it is a *salsa* made with fresh, uncooked ingredients.

Ingredients:
2 small tomatoes blanched and chopped
1 small onion finely chopped
1 *jalapeño chile* (tinned or ready frozen) and chopped
A bunch of coriander finely chopped
Salt to taste

Preparation:
Place the tomatoes, onion, coriander, *chile*, and salt in a medium sized bowl and mix well. Serve at room temperature

Cook's tip: to blanch the tomatoes, dip them in boiling water for 20 seconds or so and then immediately plunge them in cold water to stop them from cooking further.

In Mexico most people use *Knorr* or *Maggie* chicken or vegetable stock granules for their daily cooking and I often add a little to *salsas* instead of salt.

Once again my thoughts turn to Tonalá, Jalisco where Señora Alcalá always told me that *salsa* only tastes right if the tomatoes are toasted on a *comal* (griddle). We have had many conversations on the subject. Although I agree, most of us are far too busy these days. The quickest method is to blanch the tomatoes in hot water, but there is nothing to stop you following Señora Alcala's advice!

Salsa sin chile
Salsa without chile

Señora Cuca from Tonalá, Jalisco gave me this recipe for a *salsa* without *chile*. Among the things I enjoyed most about the village, during my buying trips for the shop, were my evening visits to Señora Cuca's house. All her grandchildren would gather round the table and we would play games while the *merienda* was being prepared. Sweet breads, which I love, were always served. The variety is enormous and everyone in Mexico has their favourite. These breads are like French and Danish pastries, and many were introduced during the French occupation of Mexico in the nineteenth century. Often I would go to the bakery to buy the bread with one of Señora Cuca's grandchildren while she made us hot chocolate. Her daughters in law said that their children just love to be at their grandmother's home. This is a real help to the mothers as they can get on with work in the pottery workshop knowing the children are well looked after.

With children around her table on a daily basis, Señora Cuca knows how to prepare *salsas* for the younger ones. This is the recipe she gave me. The quantity of each ingredient depends on your taste, but as a guide I use two or three tomatoes for a small onion (or a quarter of a medium sized onion).

Ingredients:
Tomatoes blanched and chopped
Garlic finely chopped
Onion finely chopped
Marjoram
Juice of a lime
A spoon of corn or vegetable oil
Salt

Preparation:
Mix all the ingredients well and serve as required.

Salsa cocida
Cooked salsa

Paty, a good friend of ours from Taxco, Guerrero, showed me how to make this *salsa* and ever since it has been affectionately known to us as 'Salsa Paty'. The *salsa* has proved very useful as it can be made in quantities and frozen it small containers to be used as needed. On my last visit to Taxco I discovered that this is a typical *salsa* that everybody makes there. The quantities depend on how much you want to make, but the basic rule is one *jalapeño chile* for every tomato and a small onion for every four tomatoes.

Ingredients:
4 tomatoes
4 *jalapeño chiles*
1 small onion
1 or 2 garlic cloves
Dried herbs (optional)
Salt to taste

Preparation:
Remove the stalk from the *chiles*. Place the onion, whole *chiles* and tomatoes in a saucepan with water and boil until the *chiles* changes colour (the *chiles* are cooked when they change colour). Leave to cool, then blend the mixture in a blender or food processor. The *salsa* is now ready for use as required. This is the time to freeze it. I use 250 gram plastic containers (old crème frâiche and yoghurt containers are a good size). Label and date the containers before freezing.

Ways to use *salsa cocida*:
-Serve as it is in a small dish and place on the table to be spooned over your meal.
-Mix with avocado pear to make a dip.
-Add to a casserole, soup or any dish you are cooking that needs a bit of extra flavour.
-Add a spoonful to any other *salsa* you are making.
-Use in any other way that takes your fancy.

Ceviche

Ingredients:

500 grams fish fillet diced

9 limes

4 tomatoes blanched and chopped

6 *jalapeño chiles* seeds removed and chopped (if using tinned *jalapeño chiles* add 3 teaspoons of the juice from the tin)

2 onions finely chopped

1 tablespoon vinegar

1 teaspoon oregano

4 tablespoons olive oil

Salt and pepper to taste

Preparation:

Wash the fish thoroughly, remove the skin and bones and dice. Marinate with the juice of 6 limes in a ceramic or plastic dish for 4 hours or over night. Stir from time to time to ensure the juice is properly absorbed. Season with salt to taste. Mix all the other ingredients together and pour over the marinated fish. Serve as a starter or *botana* with drinks.

Left: ceramic vase in the form of a fish. Tlatilco 800-400 BC.

Sopa Tarasca
Tarascan tomato soup

The Purepecha people of Pátzcuaro were called Tarascan by the Spanish and this delicious soup is named after them. The center of the Tarascan Empire was Lake Pátzcuaro and the site of Tzintzuntzán their capital city.

Ingredients:
200 grams fresh tomatoes chopped (with skin)
1 mug water
½ small onion
1 garlic clove chopped
2 *ancho chiles* soaked in water for 10 minutes
2 maize *tortillas*
1 litre chicken or vegetable stock
Sprig of *epazote*
Pinch of oregano
Corn or vegetable oil for frying
Salt to taste

For garnish:
6 maize *tortillas* cut in strips and fried
Wensleydale cheese crumbled
Crème frâiche

Preparation:
Place the tomatoes, onion, garlic, one *tortilla* and soaked *ancho chile* in a blender and puree finely. Heat some oil in a saucepan and when hot add the pureed mixture. Fry on a low heat for about 5 to 7 minutes. Add the stock and the herbs and simmer for another 10 minutes. Season to taste. Serve hot in bowls and garnish with the crème frâiche, *tortilla* strips and cheese.

Sopa de fideo
Vermicelli pasta soup

Although people do not usually think of pasta being particularly Mexican, vermicelli pasta (called *fideo* in Mexico) is very popular. This soup is often served as a starter. Children love it and even the vegetables they dislike can be disguised. Vermicelli pasta is sold in *nests* and can be found in most shops.

Ingredients:
125 grams or 2 nests *vermicelli* pasta
6 tomatoes blanched
1 small onion roughly chopped
2 garlic cloves
2 litres chicken or vegetable stock
1 sprig parsley or 5 of coriander
(I often use dried parsley with good results)
Salt to taste
Corn or vegetable oil for frying

For garnish:
Grated cheese

Preparation:
Puree the onion, garlic and tomatoes in a blender. Heat some oil in a pan and fry the *vermicelli*, crushing it in your hand as you place it in the pan. Stir and brown the *vermicelli* over low heat, taking care not to burn it. Pour in the pured mixture and fry for 3 or 4 minutes. Add the stock and bring to the boil. Simmer for 10 to 15 minutes until the *vermicelli* is tender. Stir occasionally to prevent the *vermicelli* sticking to the bottom of the pan. Serve hot and garnish with grated cheese.

Variations:
A friend of mine has had problems getting her young daughter to eat her vegetables. As she always loved my *sopa de fideo*, I suggested she boiled and pureed the vegetables with tomatoes and make the soup. It worked and now her daughter has no problem with vegetables. Of course she does not know she is eating them!

Huevos ahogados
Drowned eggs

Ingredients:
4 tomatoes
4 eggs
1 small onion
1 garlic clove
1 *jalapeño chile* chopped
Fresh coriander (parsley can also be used)
1 mug water
Corn or vegetable oil for frying
Salt to taste

Preparation:
Blanch and peel the tomatoes. Puree in a blender together with the onion and garlic. Heat two tablespoons of oil in a pan with a lid. Pour in the tomato puree and cook for a few minutes. Add the coriander or fresh herbs, the *jalapeño chile*, salt and water and boil for about 5 minutes. Lower the heat to simmering point, then drop the eggs in one by one taking care not to break the egg yolk. Place the lid on the pan and cook until the egg whites are set. Serve in small bowl.

Huevos rancheros
Eggs ranch style

Huevos rancheros make a delicious breakfast or Sunday brunch. To prepare them, lightly fry two *tortillas* and turn them onto a plate. Fry 2 eggs, place them ontop of the *tortillas* and spoon some *salsa* over them. Serve with a spoon of refried beans.

Huevos al gusto

The first time I (Anna) went to Mexico on my own, I spotted *Huevos al gusto* on a restaurant menu. I couldn't understand what all the fuss was about when I placed my order for just that. "¿Al gusto de quien?" came the reply. I had ordered "Eggs any way you like", thinking it was the name of a dish. The waiter mused over whether I'd like my eggs any way he'd like, or any way the chef would like!

Como hacer salsa de jitomate:
How to make a tomato sauce:

Ingredients:
4 tomatoes blanched and chopped
1 small onion
1 garlic clove
1 *jalapeño chile* toasted and chopped (or tinned)
A pinch of dried oregano
Fresh or dried herbs (coriander, parsley)

Preparation:
Many Mexican cookery books and magazines tell you to "make a tomato sauce" but not how to make it. This is because it is a base for many everyday dishes and it is assumed that everyone knows how to make it. Here are quick instructions for making a tomato sauce:

Fry the onion and garlic and when transparent add the chopped tomatoes and *jalapeño chile*. Cook for a few minutes and add the fresh herbs if you are using them, (or dried herbs such a mixed herbs, oregano, marjoram and parsley). I also add *Knorr* chicken or vegetable stock.

As it takes time to prepare the tomato sauce, I usually make it in large quantities. When fresh tomatoes are in season, I buy a whole box, use some for salads and the rest for sauce. I freeze it in 250/300 grams crème frâiche containers, which can then be added to other dishes as needed.

Puntas de filete a la mexicana

Ends of fillet steak Mexican style

This dish is found on most restaurant menus throughout Mexico.

Ingredients:
500 grams ends of fillet steak cut into small pieces
6 small tomatoes blanched and chopped.
1 onion finely chopped
4 *jalapeño chiles* finely chopped with stalks and seeds removed
Small bunch coriander chopped
Pinch of mixed herbs
1 garlic clove crushed
Corn or vegetable oil for frying

Preparation:
Heat two tablespoons of oil in a frying pan and when very hot fry the meat on both sides, just enough to seal the juices. Add the garlic, onion, *chiles*, tomatoes, herbs, coriander and salt to taste. Cook on low heat for about 7 minutes to season and blend the flavours. Serve with rice and refried beans.

Pescado a la Veracruzana
Fish Veracruz Style

Allow 350 grams per person when using whole fish and 150 grams when using fillet

Ingredients for the sauce:
500 grams fresh tomatoes blanched and chopped
1 onion sliced
4 garlic cloves
3 *jalapeño chiles* in brine (tinned)
100 grams olives
1 red pepper toasted and cut in strips with skin removed (or Spanish tinned *pimiento moron*)
50 grams capers
1 lime
Glass of wine (250 ml)
3 bay leaves
Oregano
Parsley
Salt and pepper to taste
Corn or vegetable oil for frying

Preparation:
Place the fish in a dish with the salt, pepper and lime juice to marinate, while you prepare the sauce. Fry the garlic cloves in a frying pan, remove them and fry the onions until transparent. Add the chopped tomatoes, fry for a couple of minutes, then pour in some of the wine. Cook for another minute. Add the fish to the sauce together with the *chiles*, red peppers, olives, herbs and the rest of the wine. Cook on a low heat until the fish is tender. Serve with rice.

Avocado pear.

Avocado

El aguacate - Ahoacatl - Persea americana

In his book *Memorandum of the Things of New Spain,* the sixteenth century Spanish friar, Bartolomé de Benavente, describes with great admiration the fields of plants and trees cultivated by the Mexican people. Among them he observed a fruit called *ahuacatl,* which grew on a tree and hung like a large fig, some ten centimeters in length. He noted five or six different varieties, some of which grew all year round. The taste was so good, he said, that he regarded it the best fruit in New Spain.

The avocado is native to Mexico and has long been recognised as a fruit with high nutritional and medicinal properties. For this reason, the Aztecs fed avocados to the infirm. The leaves of the plant were recommended for diarrhoea, the powdered peel of the fruit was used in the treatment of worms, and the oil produced from the flesh was used to heal burns.

Avocados are a rich source of vitamin B, C, E and potassium. They have the highest protein content of any fruit and are high in monounsaturated fats (thought to lower blood cholesterol levels). The only drawback is that avocados are extremely high in calories – some contain up to 400 per fruit!

From Puebla, Mexico, avocado samplings were taken to the Southern U.S.A. where they acclimatised perfectly and flourished. They grow in tropical and subtropical regions on trees of ten to fifteen meters high. Cultivation was established in California and Florida in 1932, before spreading to Israel, South Africa and Argentina. However, Mexico is still the world's main producer. As well as for general consumption, avocado flesh today is used for oil extraction and in the production of pharmaceuticals.

Most of the school children I work with describe the creamy, soft flesh of the avocado as 'slimy'. The *guacamole* I make from the fruit they unanimously describe as 'delicious', so clearly the avocado has great culinary potential, even among the fussiest of eaters! *Guacamole,* one of Mexico's most popular gastronomic delicacies today, can be traced back to ancient times. The Aztecs called this cold avocado sauce or dip *ahuacamolli,* from the word *ahuacatl* (avocado) and *molli* (sauce).

Guacamole

Guacamole

Above: volcanic stone *molcajete* (morter) used to crush ingredients for fresh *salsas* and *guacamole*.

Guacamole is a very well known *salsa* or dip and only takes a few minutes to make. It can be prepared almost at the last minute in front of your friends. The avocados must be ripe (to test ripeness, hold the avocado in the palm of your hand and feel it gently. It should give slightly when pressed). If the avocados are not ripe when you buy them, wrap them in newspaper and leave them in a warm place such as an airing cupboard or on the windowsill (not on the radiator or the avocado will blacken). This method really works: it is as if the avocado must be made to believe we live in a warmer climate. Avocado and *guacamole* have a tendency to blacken and much has been written about how to prevent this. It was my friend Lupita's head cook, at their restaurant in Oaxaca, who told me the real secret of keeping avocado green.

Cook's Tip: never use metal utensils to cut or mash the avocado: always use a wooden tool.

Once this secret was passed on to me, black avocados became a thing of the past. If you stick to wooden utensils and add lime juice to your guacamole, your avocado will stay green. It is worth passing this tip on to your friends as it is not common knowledge. Most books suggest leaving in the avocado stone, which is not as affective.

Ingredients:
2 medium avocados
1 small tomato blanched and chopped
2 tablespoons onion finely chopped
Juice of one lime
Fresh coriander finely chopped
Salt to taste

Preparation:
Remove the skin of the avocado, mash the flesh and add the juice of the lime. Stir in the tomato, onion, coriander and salt and serve at once. If you are making *salsa fresca* for the same gathering, add 2 tablespoons of *salsa* to the mashed avocado and your guacamole is ready. Remember to add the lime juice first.

Salsa cocida con aguacate
Cooked salsa with avocado

Make *salsa cocida* as described in the chapter: *Tomato*. Add an avocado to make this avocado dip.

Sopa de aguacate caliente
Hot avocado soup

Ingredients:
1 small onion
1 litre chicken or vegetable stock
2 avocados
2 tomatoes blanched
1 small bunch of coriander
Salt and pepper to taste
Corn or vegetable oil for frying

Preparation:
Fry the onion in a large saucepan until it starts to brown. Puree with the chicken stock, one avocado and the tomatoes. Return the mixture to the saucepan and boil for 10 minutes with the coriander salt and pepper. When serving, add the other avocado pear diced.

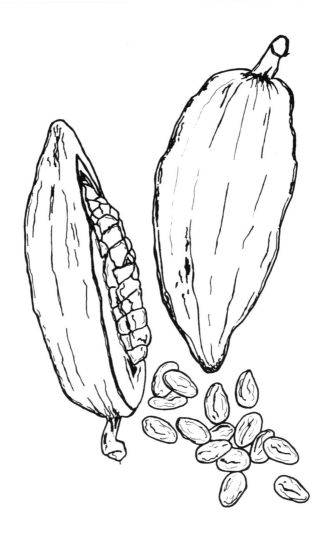

The yellow-green pods of the cocoa tree hang from the trunk and stems of the cocoa
tree (right). Each pod contains about forty beans, purple when freshly harvested,
and brown once dry and fermented. The ancient Mexicans showed great wisdom in
using their precious cocoa beans as currency: perishable treasure, that cannot be
burried or hoarded for long, discourages avaricious tendencies.

Cocoa

El cacao - Cacahoaquahuitl - Theobroma cacao

The botanical name for the most common variety of cocoa tree, *Theobroma cacoa*, means 'food of the gods'. For many people across the world, this plant certainly lives up to its name. About a billion people eat some kind of chocolate every day. Around fifty bars of one popular brand of chocolate are consumed every second in the United Kingdom alone! We have Mexico to thank for cocoa, yet few people are aware that its history dates back many centuries and that chocolate bars are a relatively new phenomenon.

Cocoa in Ancient Mexico

The history of chocolate in Mexico begins some 3000 years ago on the hot, humid plains of the Veracruz Gulf Coast. Here cocoa trees grew in the wild. The Olmecs (1500 BC - 400 AD), who established the first great civilisation of ancient Mexico, were probably the first to devise a technique to extract bitter cocoa from the cocoa bean.

Below: cocoa tree of the South. A detail from the first page of the Aztec Codex Féjerváry-Mayer. The page depicts nine gods and four world trees, which mark the cardinal points of the universe. 1350 AD.

However, little archaeological evidence has survived in this tropical environment. Linguists tell us that the word 'cocoa' (pronounced *kakawa*) may be derived from an ancient form of the Mixe-Zoquean language in use at the time. Popoluca Indians who live in this area today have preserved a form of this language.

The Maya (200 BC-1550 AD) inherited cocoa from their ancestors: they used roasted cocoa beans, water and spice to make a variety of beverages. Lowland forest was cleared to establish the earliest known cocoa plantations in about 600 AD.

Above: the Mixtec King 8 Deer receives a cup of foaming cocoa from his bride Princess 13 Serpent. Illustation from a detail of Codex Nuttal.

These extended from the province of Acalán, along the Gulf Coast of Mexico, to the Pacific Coast from Guatemala to El Salvador. In Itzamkanac, the capital of Acalán, temples were dedicated to the god Ek Chuah, patron of cocoa producers and merchants. Cocoa fruits were used at festivals in his honour.

For the Maya, cocoa had religious and spiritual significance. In the Popol Vuh, their creation myth, cocoa is one of the substances used by the gods to create the flesh of man. The fruit of the cocoa plant may have been a symbol for the human heart and liquid cocoa for the blood of man. Cocoa beans were also given as gifts at important ceremonies such as those marking the passage from boyhood to manhood.

Cocoa became an important trading commodity and the beans were used as a form of currency. Maya traders traveled far and wide with their cocoa beans. Some transported them in wooden canoes and others in large baskets strapped to the back. Wealthier traders, who had porters, ventured far and were probably the first to introduce cocoa to the Aztecs in the Valley of Mexico.

The Maya word for cocoa, *cacau,* is likely to have

come from the root *cau, chauc* or *chac* meaning 'ray' and is associated with the concept of fire, strength and the colour red. This is consistent with the energising properties of cocoa and the red colour of its shell. The Maya word *cacau* became *cacahuatl* in the Aztec language, meaning 'bitter water'.

The Aztecs considered cocoa a true delicacy, perhaps more so because they were unable to grow it themselves in the moderate climate of their capital. They ground their cherished cocoa beans into a paste and mixed them with *chile*, vanilla and honey to prepare a drink called *chocolatl*. The last emperor Moctezuma, who was particularly fond of the beverage, is said to have consumed as many as fifty portions a day. He was served in a golden goblet, poured from a height to create a frothy foam. *Chocolatl* was a luxury beverage, consumed only by nobility, warriors and the *pochteca* or long distance traders.

Initially, to satisfy their demand for cocoa, the Aztecs traded with the major cocoa producers on the Gulf and Pacific Coasts. Once these areas became part of the vast Aztec empire, the inhabitants were required to pay tribute to the capital. Records of tribute paid to the Aztecs are depicted in the Codex Mendoza, housed today in the Bodleian Library in Oxford. This revealing manuscript was commissioned by the first Spanish viceroy of Mexico, Don Antonio de Mendoza, who served from 1535-1551. The codex was written by a native artist in the Aztec pictographic language. On one page, among other items, baskets of cocoa beans are depicted, topped with white flags. The flags represent twenty loads each, bringing the total on the page to two hundred loads. The Aztecs used cocoa beans as a form of currency, together with other luxury goods such as quills filled with gold dust, lengths of cloth, copper sheets and quetzal feathers. A rabbit might go for 30 cocoa beans and a slave for 400. A *xiquipilli* or sack containing 8000 cocoa beans was used for large scale transactions.

The Florentine Codex, written by the Spanish friar Benardino de Sahagún (1499-1590), provides an insight into how cocoa was prepared and traded. In the great Aztec

Below: 100 loads of cocoa tribute, as depicted in the Aztec codex Mendoza. Each flag represents 20 loads.

markets of Tenochtitlán and Tlatelolco, there were women who sold different varieties of hot chocolate beverages, brewed with *chile*, vanilla and honey. Other vendors sold the raw beans. Honest traders separated their cocoa beans according to quality. Dishonest traders, on the other hand, had a host of tricks up their sleeve to produce 'counterfeit beans'. These might be the shells of real beans filled with earth, clay, amaranth dough or avocado seeds. Some even painted beans of inferior quality. Strict penalties were brought upon those who engaged in such illegal practises. There were judges or market officials who supervised the sale of produce: they saw that correct weights and measures were being used and that price matched quality.

Christopher Columbus and the first European Encounter with Cocoa

The first European to encounter cocoa was Christopher Columbus. On his final voyage to the Americas in 1502, Columbus and his crew seized a large native vessel off the coast of present day Honduras. Clearly the Spaniards were more amazed at the size of this enormous boat than by its cargo of local goods, for they remarked that the vessel was '*as long as a galley*'. The only hint that these *almonds*, as they referred to them, were valuable, came when the locals boarded the Spanish ship and scrambled to pick up any fallen beans. Of course the Spaniards were totally unaware then that these people were simply gathering up the local currency. Back in Spain the value of cocoa beans was totally overlooked. No one knew what to do with them in any case.

From the Aztec capital to Europe

Cocoa made a bigger impact twenty years later, this time in the form a beverage. The first Europeans to taste chocolate were Hernan Cortés and his men, in the Aztec capital of Tenochtitlán in 1519. The Spanish chronicler Bernal Díaz del Castillo observed that the emperor Moctezuma "*was served in cup shaped vessels of pure gold, a certain drink made from cocoa*" and that once he had dined his entourage were provided with "*over two thousand jugs of cocoa all frothed up*". Although

the Spaniards reportedly found the drink an acquired taste, Cortés later wrote to King Charles I, of Spain, extolling the virtues of a drink called *xocoatl* that built up resistance and fought fatigue.

A Spanish monk named Fray Aguilar, who travelled with Cortés to Mexico, may have sent back the first cocoa samples, together with a recipe for preparing hot cocoa. The monks of the Piedra monastery in Aragon may therefore have been the first to consume cocoa in Europe. The popularity of the drink increased when the recipe was altered and sugar replaced the *chile* pepper used by the Aztecs. Nonetheless cocoa remained a Spanish secret for about a hundred years until a Florentine named Antonio Carletti introduced it to Italy in 1606. Cocoa spread to France in 1615 with the marriage of Philip III's daughter, Anna of Austria, to Louis XIII of France. From there cocoa spread to England, Germany and Holland and soon became a popular luxurious beverage among the nobility of Europe.

Chocolate bars were not produced until the nineteenth century, after Dutch chocolate maker Conrad Van Houten developed a process for pressing the fat from cocoa beans in 1828. The pulverised cocoa could then be mixed with sugar and remixed with the cocoa butter to create a bar.

Pure Chocolate Heaven

I have to admit that this is one chapter of our book I have really enjoyed researching. For me, there is nothing more exquisite than a piece of fine Swiss or Belgian chocolate. I am a self confessed chocoholic and frequently crave chunky bars of chocolate, delicate pralines and chocolate chip cookies. Despite the popularity of the edible varieties of chocolate, it is worth remembering that most of chocolate's history (90% of it) relates to the drinkable variety. Even today, most of the chocolate consumed in Mexico and Latin America is served as a beverage.

Arnold Ismach makes an interesting point in his book 'The Darker Side of Chocolate', when he maintains that the 'evil' people associate with chocolate relates only to milk chocolate, which he regards as contaminated. The closer you

get to the pure variety, he maintains, (from roasted cocoa beans), the more satisfying, the safer and healthier chocolate is. With this in mind, and in an attempt to bring history to life, we have included a recipe for the preparation of a hot chocolate drink, similar to one the Maya and Aztecs used to drink. If you live in the United Kingdom, finding raw cocoa beans will be next to impossible (unless you work in the cocoa industry), but the process is interesting to read about. I tried this with a precious kilo of cocoa beans I bought in La Merced market in Mexico City.

Chocolate estilo Maya

Mayan hot chocolate

Ingedients:
500 grams cocoa beans
600 ml boiling water
Fresh *chiles*
Vanilla pod
Honey

Preparation:
Chop some *chiles*, place them in a bowl and pour the boiling water over them. Leave to infuse. Meanwhile, roast the cocoa beans on a griddle or metal pan, stirring them until they crackle and bitter oil begins to seep through. According to Tita in Laura Esquivel's novel 'Like Water for Chocolate', if you toast the beans any less, the chocolate will be indigestible: toast them any more and they will burn. While the beans are hot, peel them as quickly as possible (they are harder to peel when they are cold). Grind the beans well with a pestle and mortar. With your hands, make a long thick roll with the paste and cut in slices (about a centimeter thick). Place the cocoa tablets on a tray with greaseproof

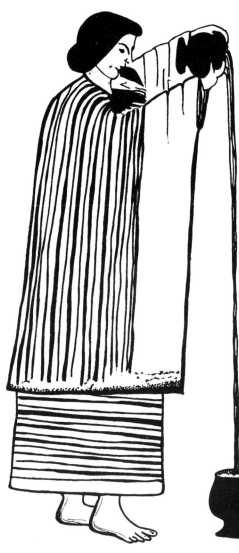

Below: an Aztec woman pours hot cocoa from a height to create foam. Codex Tudela.

paper and leave them to dry. They can then be made into a delicious hot drink.

Place 100 grams of the chocolate paste in a pan with some of the *chile* water. Bring to the boil over a medium heat, stirring constantly, until all the chocolate dissolves. Add a vanilla pod and some honey. Boil the mixture, stirring continuously. As soon as it starts to bubble, remove from the heat and allow to cool slightly. Then place back on the heat and boil again, stirring rigorously. Repeat the cooling and re-boiling several times, as this will enrich the flavour. Remove the vanilla pod. Taste the mixture and add more water and honey if necessary. Pour the liquid from one container to another back and forth (to create foam) and serve from a height to increase the froth.

Chocolate mexicano
Mexican hot chocolate

Ingredients:
1 circular tablet of Mexican spiced chocolate, such as the *Ibarra* brand or 100 grams plain chocolate (note the flavour will be different)
About 600 ml (1 pint) milk
1 tablespoon vanilla sugar
½ teaspoon of powdered cinnamon
Sugar to taste (if using plain chocolate)

Preparation:
Heat the chocolate, milk, vanilla, cinnamon and sugar in a saucepan. As the chocolate starts to dissolve, mix well.
Bring to the boil, then simmer. Whisk the mixture with a *molinillo* whisk, between the palms of your hands. Serve the chocolate when foamy.

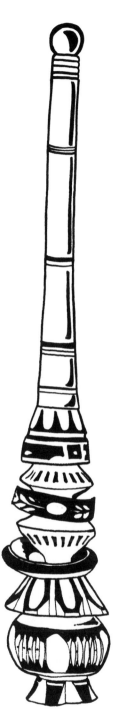

Right: hand carved *molinillo* whisk, used to froth hot chocolate. The stick is placed in the chocolate pan and rubbed briskly between the palms of the hands to create foam.

Mousse de chocolate
Heavenly mousse

Of all the products introduced from Mexico to the rest of the world, chocolate is without doubt one of the most appreciated. With this in mind I created this dessert for my restaurant – my own personal homage to chocolate. The dessert was christened by our good friend Susan (another self proclaimed chocoholic!). She describes the sensation one spoonful of mousse has on the palate. All of my guests agree! The dessert is an instant hit with all of them, who frequently taste all the desserts I offer them.

Ingredients:

250 grams *mascarpone* cheese
100 grams plain chocolate (70% cocoa)
4 eggs separated
6 tablespoons sugar
1 teaspoon gelatine
2 tablespoons strong cold coffee
50 ml *kalhua* coffee liqueur

Preparation:

Place two tablespoons of cold coffee in a small saucepan and sprinkle the gelatine granules over it. An important rule to remember when using gelatine is that it must always be added to the liquid (liquid should not be added to the gelatine). Wait until the gelatine has absorbed all the liquid.

Meanwhile separate the egg whites and yolks. Beat the egg whites with an electric mixer until they form stiff peaks. Add two tablespoons of the sugar and whip for a few more seconds. Note that to whip egg whites the blades of the mixer must be clean and dry or the whites will not whip properly. Whipping the whites first and then the yolks saves you having to wash the blades in between (the yolks can be whipped after the whites without washing in between).

Whip the egg yolks in a separate bowl with 4 tablespoons of sugar until light and creamy. Mix the *mascarpone* cheese with the yolks until the consistency is even.

Now the gelatine should be ready. Heat it gently until it dissolves, stirring fast as you do so, but do not allow to boil. Pour the coffee liqueur over the dissolved gelatine and stir, then pour the liquid into the egg yolk and cheese mixture. Next dissolve the chocolate: I do this by placing it in a dish in the microwave for a couple of minutes. Alternatively, place the chocolate in a bowl over a saucepan of hot water and heat until the chocolate dissolves. Now add the chocolate to the egg yolk and *mascarpone* cheese mixture. Fold the whipped egg whites into the mixture with a metal spoon, taking care not to loose air. Pour the chocolate mixture into individual dessert dishes or a large dish and place in the fridge to set.

Variations:

I use Italian *mascarpone* cheese as it is rich and creamy, but less heavy and more refreshing than cream. You can also substitute the *mascapone* cheese for crème frâiche. If you have more guests and do not want to increase the amounts used, line your serving dishes with strawberries or any other fruit you like and then pour the chocolate mixture on top.

Left: Cup of cocoa, Codex Mendoza.

Cocoa 169

Flowering vanilla orchid and pod.

Vanilla

La vainilla - Tlixcóchitl - Vanilla planifolia

Vanilla, an exquisite plant belonging to the orchid family, is another product of Mexican origin. Today vanilla is used mainly as flavouring for liqueurs, chocolate, cakes, biscuits and sweets. It is also used to disguise the taste of disagreeable medicines. Like many orchids, vanilla is a parasite that usually grows on the trunks of other trees, sheltered under the jungle canopy. The Aztecs named vanilla *tlilxochitl* or 'black flower' from the words *tliltic* meaning 'black' and *xochitl* for 'flower'. They used vanilla to flavour a hot chocolate drink, which the Spaniards tried for the first time at the palace of Moctezuma. Very much taken with the flavour, the Spanish were quick to transport vanilla back to Europe. The word *vanilla* comes from the Spanish word *vaina* meaning 'sheath', *vanilla* being 'small sheath'.

Vanilla was discovered by the Totonac people in Eastern Mexico in what is today the state of Veracruz and part of Puebla. The Totonac name for the plant was also 'black flower' or *xanath* in their language. Vanilla requires specific conditions in which to grow; a hot, humid climate and not more than five hundred meters in altitude. The Totonac region provided perfect conditions and today the best quality vanilla is still produced in Veracruz.

For the Totonac, vanilla was a symbol of life and central to their religion, in the same way that maize was significant to other Mesoamerican cultures. Legend holds that vanilla was created by a young princess named Tzacopontziza or 'morning star'. Today the Totonac still grow vanilla with almost religious dedication and some keep a few vines in their houses for good luck.

At the annual vanilla festival, this precious crop is celebrated. Vanilla pods are delicately woven into baskets and figures such as frogs and insects. The famous *voladores* or flying dancers of Papantla perform an astonishing feat, which dates back to pre-Hispanic times: four *voladores* (flyers), who represent the four cardinal points of the earth, and a musician, climb to the top of a fifteen meter pole, winding a long rope around it as they ascend. At the top, with the rope tied only to their wastes, the *voladores* jump off spectacularly and fly around the pole. As the twisted rope unravels, they gradually descend to the ground.

The process involved in the cultivation and preparation of vanilla is laborious and delicate. Mexico is the only place in the world where vanilla is pollinated in the wild by hummingbirds and a bee called Melipona. Elsewhere, and when grown as a crop, human intervention is required. In the Totonac region young women were traditionally given the delicate job of climbing the trees to pollinate the flowers. In Springtime, hundreds of young girls, dressed in white, could be seen fluttering across the countryside like butterflies. When the work was done, the vanilla *fiesta* began.

Above: flat stamp hummingbird motif found in Yucatán. By Jorge Enciso. Vanilla flowers in Mexico are pollinated in the wild by bees and humming-birds. Elsewhere in the world, away from their natural habitat, the flowers must be pollinated by hand.

At harvest time, the ripe fruit or 'stick' is cut and spread out on straw mats to dry in the sun. In the late afternoon the vanilla is covered, so that it retains heat and sweats, which concentrates the aroma. The sticks are sorted and rotten or diseased fruits are discarded. The whole process is repeated for several weeks.

Mexico monopolized vanilla production until the nineteenth century. As cultivation increased elsewhere in the world, the demand for Mexican vanilla decreased. Although the quality is slightly inferior, vanilla is now cultivated in Madagascar, Mauritius, Indonesia, Tahiti and tropical America. A method of producing vanilla artificially in a laboratory has now been developed. Although the flavour is inferior the price is more appealing to industry, making the future for producers of natural vanilla uncertain. However, many people appreciate the taste and aroma of quality natural vanilla, so there will hopefully always be a demand for it.

The last time my mother purchased a vanilla pod at our local supermarket, thousands of miles away from the village of Papantla, the girl at the cashier was more than curious. "Would you mind telling me what this is?" she asked. She had never seen a vanilla pod and was intrigued to hear how my mother makes her own vanilla sugar. Many of the children and teachers I work with have never seen vanilla pods either. They are often surprised that this small stick from Mexico is the source of such sweet aroma and flavour.

Como hacer azucar de vainilla
How to make vanilla sugar

Ingredients:
1 vanilla pod
Caster sugar

Preparation:
Fill a glass jar with caster sugar and insert the vanilla pod. Place the lid back on the jar and store in your kitchen cupboard. After a few weeks, depending on the strength of the vanilla pod, the sugar will absorb the flavour of the pod.

Left: vanilla pod and flower.

Pastel Aleman de manzana
German apple cake

Vanilla sugar is used widely in German baking recipes and there are many recipes for apple cakes which use vanilla. I have included this recipe as it is the first cake I ever made in my life. While I was living on a farm in Germany, my friend Sigrid Mayer, her mother Oma Elli, her mother-in-law Oma Tasser, and Malis the house keeper, took so much care to teach me and shared their vast knowledge of German cake making. This set the foundations and began my life long enthusiasm for baking. This is the only cake I can make totally from memory without having to measure ingredients, so I will do my best to describe the process.

Ingredients:
250 grams self-raising flour or plain flour with baking powder
125 grams butter or margarine
125 grams sugar
1 large egg or two small ones
6 apples depending on size (I use whichever are in season)
1 tablespoon of vanilla sugar
Pinch of salt
Flaked almonds for the topping

Equipment:
24 or 26 cm diameter spring form baking tin
Preparation:
Pre-heat the oven to 190°C, 350°F, Gas Mark 5. Grease the baking tin. Peel and cut the apples in fine slices and set aside. In a large bowl, mix the flour, sugar, vanilla sugar, butter or margarine and salt with your hands until it resembles crumbs. It is important to incorporate air into the pastry or dough. Add the eggs one at a time, reserving half an egg yolk for the topping. Work the mixture into the dough. Place just over half the dough in the tin and mould into the base of the tin with your fingers. Arrange the sliced apples ontop. Roll the rest of the dough with a rolling pin and cover the apples (any left over dough makes delicious biscuits).

For the topping mix the half egg yolk with a spoon of milk. Brush it over the cake and sprinkle with flaked almonds. Alternatively top with small pieces of butter or sprinkle with sugar as soon as you take the cake out of the oven. Bake in the middle of a hot oven for about 45 to 60 minutes at 190°C /350°F/Gas Mark 5.

Crema planchada
Crème brûlée

Ingredients:
4 egg yolks
400 ml double cream
1 vanilla pod split lengthways or vanilla essence
4 teaspoons caster sugar (or vanilla sugar instead of the caster sugar and vanilla)
Sugar for the caramel topping

Allow one egg yolk per person. Use 100 ml double cream and one teaspoon of caster sugar per egg yolk.

Preparation:
Pour the cream into a saucepan and add the vanilla pod (if using one). Heat but do not allow to boil. Remove from the heat and leave the vanilla to infuse (for about ten minutes). Meanwhile beat the egg yolks and sugar in a bowl until the mixture lightens and thickens. Pour the hot cream into the egg mixture, whipping until all are blended together.

If using vanilla essence add it now. Return the cream and egg yolk mixture to the pan. Place the pan over another pan of hot but not boiling water. Continue stirring until the mixture thickens enough to coat the back of a spoon thickly. Remove the vanilla pod and pour the custard into small cups. Leave to cool and keep in the fridge until set.

Pre-heat the grill to very hot. Sprinkle some caster sugar on top of the custard and place the cups under a hot grill to caramelise. If you have one, use a chef's gas torch instead. They are fun to use and quicker and easier than placing under the grill. Leave to cool and set before serving.

Helado de vainilla
Vanilla ice cream

Ice cream making used to be a regular routine for me in the early seventies when my children were young. When we returned to the United Kingdom from Singapore, my son Alexander was two years old. He decided he did not like hot meals and only wanted to eat ice cream: so I set myself the task of making real ice cream with fresh fruit to add more nutrients.

Ice cream is popular in Mexico and is usually made with real fruit. Ice cream parlours and *paleterias* are a common sight. Many are called 'La Michoacana' after the state of Michoacán, which is famous for its ice cream. Tiring of my endless research into local pottery, my daughter Anna once spent a whole afternoon at a huge ice cream stall in Oaxaca city market. The vendor was quite happy to let her try all the unusual flavours. These included tropical fruits that are common in Mexico such as *mamey, guayava, papaya* and *zapote*. Other more unusual flavours included avocado, maize and *chile*. Today vanilla is one of the most popular flavours for ice cream throughout the world.

Ingredients:
500 ml milk
500 ml double cream whipped
6 eggs whites and yolks separated
1 vanilla pod or vanilla essence
Pinch of salt

Preparation:
Place the milk, sugar and vanilla pod (or essence) in a saucepan. Remove from the heat when boiling. Whip the egg yolks and add some of the hot milk as you whip. Pour this mixture into the rest of the milk. Place over a low heat and whisk with a metal hand whisk until the custard thickens. When cool, pour into a large bowl and place in the freezer.

When the custard starts to freeze add the whipped double cream, mix both very well and place back in the freezer. Whip two egg whites until stiff (as when making meringues). One hour later, take the custard out of the freezer and fold in the egg whites thoroughly. At this stage you can divide the ice cream to make different flavours (for example by mixing in fruit or chocolate).

For chocolate ice cream, add 200 grams of melted bitter chocolate. For strawberry ice cream, mash strawberries with sugar and mix with the vanilla ice cream. Place back in the freezer until needed.

Ceramic pot with green glaze, in the form of a pineapple. San José de Gracia, Michoacán.

Desserts and Cakes

Postres y Pasteles

Flan napolitano o flan de tres leches
Neapolitan crème caramel or
Three milks crème caramel

Ingredients:
1 - 400 gram tin condensed sweetened milk
1 - 400 gram tin evaporated milk
Fresh milk (use one of the empty tins to measure)
6 eggs
2 tablespoons of brandy

N.B. The exact measurements of the tinned milk are not important (e.g. 380g/410g). What maters is the proportion of eggs to liquid.

For the caramel:
Sugar and a little water (I never measure the sugar but I use about 4 tablespoons)

Preparation:
Pre-heat the oven to 150°C, 300°F, Gas Mark 2. To make the caramel, heat the sugar and a little water in a small pan. Boil until the sugar caramelises, taking care not to burn it, as this will leave a bitter flavour. Pour into an ovenproof dish and set aside.

Meanwhile mix all the other ingredients together, by hand or with a blender. If mixing by hand, whisk the eggs first, then add the condensed milk, the evaporated milk, the fresh milk and finally the brandy (it is easier to mix the thick liquids first).

Pour the liquid mixture into the caramel dish. Place the dish in a baking pan of water (at least half way up the dish) and bake in the oven *bain-marie*. Cook for about an hour at 150°C /300°F/ Gas Mark 2. Test the caramel by inserting a long baking needle into the centre. If the needle comes out clean the caramel is cooked. Set aside to cool, then chill. It is better to make the caramel a day or two before you need it as the caramel dissolves better.

To serve:

To turn the caramel over pass a knife between the dish and the caramel, to free it from the dish. Place a plate on top and turn over carefully. Scrape any caramel from the mould into the serving dish.

Flan (caramel) variations

Flans or caramels were a treat for me as a child as far back as I can remember. You can make them any way you like providing you have the right balance of eggs and liquid. 4 eggs are usually enough, but I often use 6 eggs to make the caramel larger. This gives you some left over for the next day!

When I was young, I used to go to lunch at a restaurant in Coyoacán, Mexico City called '*El Coyote Flaco*' (the Skiny Coyote). The food was excellent and the caramel was delicious. The waiter knew about my passion for *flan* so I was always given huge helpings. During those early days I was not interested in cooking: I just enjoyed eating, so it never occurred to me to ask for the recipe. But the aromas and flavour stayed with me for life.

One day not long ago, I discovered a 400 ml tub of natural yoghurt in the fridge. It had just passed its *best before* date. Not wanting it to go to waste, I decided to use it for cooking. I made a *flan* with a tin of sweetened condensed milk, a tin of evaporated milk, the tub of yoghurt, 6 eggs and brandy.

With the first bite the memories came flooding back. The caramel tasted just the same as the one I had enjoyed so much many years ago in '*El Coyote Flaco*'. I do not know if the place still exists after 35 years, but the memories will stay with me forever.

Variations with cream, cheese or yoghurt

Substitute the tin of evaporated milk or the fresh milk for fresh cream, crème frâiche, natural or fruit yoghurt (400 ml), *mascarpone* cheese, or any other cream cheese you like.

Fruit caramels

Fruit caramels make refreshing desserts on long summer days and are easy and economical to make. They contain no milk: use 6 eggs for ½ litre of juice.

Ingredients:
500 ml fruit juice (or tinned fruit pureed, and juice to make the liquid up to 500 ml)
100 grams sugar when using orange or pineapple juice (no extra sugar is needed if tinned fruit is used as they contain enough)
6 eggs
2 tablespoons brandy or rum depending of which fruit you use. Rum goes well with most tropical fruits.

I have used strawberries for this recipe and they taste great: however, they go dark brown when cooked so are less appealing to the eye.

Preparation:
Pre-heat the oven to 150°C, 300°F, Gas Mark 2. To make the caramel heat the sugar and a little water in a small pan. Boil until the sugar caramelises, taking care not to burn it as this will leave a bitter flavour. Pour into an ovenproof dish and set aside.

Whip the eggs then mix in the other ingredients (or mix all the ingredients in a blender). Pour the mixture into the caramel dish. Place the dish in a baking pan of water (at least half way up the dish) and bake in the oven *bain-marie* for about 60 minutes at 150°C, 300°F, Gas Mark 2. Check the caramel is cooked by inserting a kitchen needle or knife. If the knife comes out clean the caramel is ready.

Flan de merengue
Meringue caramel

Ingredients:
200 grams caster sugar (20 grams of sugar per egg)
10 egg whites
1 teaspoon vanilla essence
½ teaspoon cream of tartar
Pinch of salt

For the caramel:
200 grams sugar
50 ml water
½ teaspoon vanilla essence
¼ teaspoon almond essence

For the cream topping:
250 ml whipping or double cream
100 grams toasted flaked almonds
1 tin mango or any other fruit you like

For the alternative yoghurt topping:
250 ml double cream
Natural yoghurt
100 grams toasted flaked almonds
2 or 3 spoons of caster sugar to taste (optional)

Preparation:
Preheat the oven to 180°C, 350°F, Gas Mark 4. To make the caramel, heat the sugar and a little water in a small pan. Boil until the sugar caramelises, taking care not to burn it, as this will leave a bitter flavour. Add the vanilla and almond essence. Pour into a ring mould and tilt to cover the sides and bottom of the mould. Set aside and when cool butter the uncovered areas.

Whip the egg whites, salt and cream of tarter in a large bowl until the egg white is glossy and forms stiff peaks. Fold in the caster sugar and add the vanilla and almond essence. Pour the meringue into the caramel-coated mould. Place the dish in a baking pan of water (at least half way up the dish) and bake *bain-marie* for 45-60 minutes. When

cooked, turn off the oven, leaving the caramel inside for 10 minutes, with the door open. Handle the meringue carefully: a strong draft or loud noise (such as banging the oven door) might upset the meringue.

After 10 minutes take the caramel out of the oven and leave to cool at room temperature. Do not expose to strong changes of temperature. When cool (after about 20 minutes) turn onto a large plate and scrape off as much of the caramel as you can from the mould. If the mould is metal, add a little water and heat the dish on the cooker to melt the caramel. If the dish is *Pyrex* ™ add the water and heat in the oven or microwave to melt. Pour the melted caramel into a small jug or dish, allowing it to cool before pouring it over the meringue. Sprinkle with toasted flaked almonds.

Cream topping:
Whip the cream and pile in the middle of the meringue, with the fruit. The meringue can be made the day before, ready to add the cream and fruit one or two hours before serving.

Alternative yoghurt topping:
Whip the double cream until it stands in peaks, fold in the yoghurt (about 5 or 6 tablespoons) and use as for the cream topping.

Arroz con leche
Rice pudding

Mexican rice pudding is much quicker and more economical to make than the traditional British rice pudding, which is baked in the oven for a long time (in the old days in Britain when rice puddings were cooked slowly in the Aga, this was more economical on fuel. The Aga had the dual function of heating the household). If you do not normally like rice pudding, try this Mexican version.

Ingredients:

250 grams (1 mug) Italian pudding rice (short grain)
You can use long grain but short grain absorbs the milk better and creates a more creamy texture
2 ½ to 3 mugs water
Pinch of salt
Cinnamon stick
1 litre milk
6 tablespoons sugar (about 100 grams) to taste

Preparation:

Wash the rice under running water in a colander. Place in a large saucepan with the water, cinnamon and a pinch of salt. Cook on low heat for about 20 minutes, or until tender. Remove any excess water left in the pan. Add the litre of milk and the sugar, stirring continuously. Bring to the boil and cook for 5 to 10 minutes more, stirring continuously. Pour into a large ceramic dish and leave to set. The rice will absorb the milk as it sets.

Variations:

For a special treat add a small glass of sherry to the pan before pouring into the dish. Add two egg yolks, with a little of the hot milk, towards the end for a creamier custard texture. You can also add sultanas or raisins.

Arroz de tres leches
Three milks rice pudding

Tinned milks are very popular in Mexico. Cows were introduced to Mexico by the Spanish in the sixteenth century, but fresh milk was not so readily available, partly due to the climate. Hundreds of years later, tinned milk provided an alternative. Nowadays everybody has a fridge and milk is plentiful in supermarkets. Even the smaller villages have a shop selling fresh milk. However, tinned milks are very popular for making desserts like this one.

Ingredients:
1 mug pudding rice
2 to 3 mugs water
1 cinnamon stick
¼ teaspoon salt
2 mugs fresh milk
1 tin evaporated milk
1 tin condensed milk
Raisins for decoration (optional)

Preparations:
Wash the rice under running water in a colander, then cook it with the water and cinnamon stick for about 20 minutes, or until tender. Check that all the water has been absorbed, then add the fresh milk, salt and evaporated milk. Boil for a few minutes, stirring well. Add the condensed, sweetened milk and continue to stir for a couple of minutes. Pour the rice pudding into a dish and when cool decorate with the raisins.

Nieve de piña

Pineapple snow

Ingredients:
½ litre double cream
425 grams tinned pineapple or any other fruit you like such as mangos or apricots (if using dried apricots, soak them overnight first)
90 grams sugar
6 egg yolks

Preparation:
Puree the fruit with its syrup and heat in a small saucepan. Bring to the boil and turn off the heat. Whip the egg yolks a little and set aside. Heat the cream and sugar in a saucepan on a low heat, stirring continuously. When hot, spoon some of the cream into the whipped egg yolk. Add this mixture to the saucepan and cook until the mixture thickens, stirring all the time, but do not allow it to boil. Turn off the heat and pour the warmed fruit mixture (or fruit) into the custard, stirring as you do so.

Pour the custard into dessert dishes and when cool decorate with pieces of pineapple. This dessert can be made the day before and kept in the fridge until served.

Right: ceramic plate, Talavera, Puebla.

Jericalla de melon
Melon custard pudding

On all my bus journeys from village to village, in Mexico, I hear the cries of ladies selling *jericallas* at the bus stops. *Jericallas* are delicious home made puddings. This one is made with melon and is very economical during the summer when *Galia* melons are in season.

Ingredients:
250 grams Galia melon cut in pieces
500 ml milk
100 grams sugar
4 egg yolks
2 egg whites
50 grams toasted flaked almonds
1 stick cinnamon
Pinch of ground cinnamon
Butter to grease the dishes

Preparation:
Pre-heat the oven to 160°C, 300°F, Gas Mark 2. Puree the melon with a little of the milk and mix in a saucepan with the remaining milk, sugar and cinnamon stick. Boil for 3 minutes and leave to cool a little.

Meanwhile, beat the egg whites and yolks and pour into the milk and melon mixture. Pour the mixture into a ready greased dish or small individual ones. Place the dish in a baking pan of water and bake *bain-marie* for 30 minutes at 160°C, 300°F, Gas Mark 2 if you are using individual moulds and longer if you are using a single larger dish (about 1 hour).

Platanos borrachos
Drunken bananas

Ingredients:
6 bananas
50 grams plain flour
50 grams unsalted butter
50 grams sugar
2 oranges cut in pieces zest and peel removed
120 ml rum
1 lime
Pinch of cinnamon

Preparation:
Make 60 ml of sugar syrup *(jarabe be azucar)* by boiling 120 ml of water and 2 tablespoons of sugar, until the quantity is reduced by half.

Pre-heat the oven to 180°C, 350°F, Gas Mark 4. Peel the bananas and spread with the butter. Mix together the flour and sugar and coat the bananas with them. Grease an ovenproof dish. Place the bananas in the dish and arrange the oranges over them. Mix the rum, syrup and limejuice and pour over the bananas. Sprinkle with cinnamon and cook in the microwave for 8 minutes. To bake in the oven, heat to 180°C, 350°F, Gas Mark 4 and bake for 30 minutes.

Cajeta
Cajeta syrup

When Mexicans go abroad for long periods, particularly to study, one of the things they miss is *cajeta*. I have been asked countless times to bring back jars of *cajeta*, yet it is so simple to make. However, you rarely think of making something yourself, if it is easily found on the supermarket shelf.

Here is a basic recipe of mine for *cajeta*:

Ingredients:
2 litres goats milk plus 125 ml for the honey
1 teaspoon vanilla essence or cinnamon
1 teaspoon bicarbonate of soda
1¼ kilos sugar
125 ml maize syrup, known in Mexico as *miel de maiz*. I have used bee's honey. I have not tested other syrups, but they would probably do. Some specialist shops stock *Karo,* a Mexican maize syrup.

To make the cajeta:
Pour 2 litres of milk into a large (about 3 litre capacity) saucepan with the vanilla and bicarbonate of soda. Bring to the boil and set aside. Mix the sugar with 125 ml of milk in another smaller pan and boil until the colour turns golden. Pour this into the milk mixture in the larger saucepan, together with the maize syrup or honey. Mix well and bring to the boil. Simmer for approximately 45 minutes, stirring constantly to avoid the mixture sticking to the bottom of the pan and burning. Continue until the mixture thickens, comes off the spoon in a continuous thread and the bottom of the saucepan is visible while stirring. Remove from the heat and leave to cool.The *cajeta* can be stored in glass jam jars to be used as a spread on bread, with waffles, pancakes or poured onto puddings.

Cajeta almendrada
Almond cajeta syrup

Ingredients:
200 grams almonds blanched and toasted
2 litres milk
750 grams sugar
7 egg yolks beaten
1 cup sweet sherry
1 teaspoon ground cinnamon

Preparations:
Grind half of the almonds in a grinder and mix them with the milk and the sugar. Heat the mixture in a saucepan on a low heat and bring to the boil, stirring continuously until the *cajeta* starts to thicken. Remove the pan from the heat and add the beaten egg yolks. Return to the cooker and cook for 15 minutes, stirring constantly. Add the cherry and cinnamon little by little, stirring continuously at simmering point until you can see the bottom of the pan.

Spoon into a dish and decorate with the rest of the almonds.

Right: sunflower design from a ceramic plate, Dolores Hidalgo, Guanajuato.

Cakes in my life

There is a contrast in Mexico that still puzzles me: delicious, home made cakes are sold everywhere, yet people seem to store their pots and pans in the oven (ovens are rarely used). Perhaps because homemade cakes can be bought so easily, most people do not bother to make them. Hence how impressed I was during my early years as a Forces wife, with all the British wives I met who would make cakes for tea parties. Having worked in the city, I had no idea how to put a cake together. I felt quite inadequate! Things were not improved by the fact that every time I asked about baking or made a compliment, I would always be told, "but it's so easy, it tells you in the book." So my knowledge was not improved.

It was my German friends in Hameln, the land of the Pied Piper, who spared the time to teach me how to bake from their old books in their wonderful traditional kitchens. They wanted to make a real country girl of me. They also told me that the reason my runner beans grew all over the place was because they needed poles to support them!

During my early trips back to Mexico to buy for my shop, one of the places I visited most was Tonalá in Jalisco. During those early years there was only one restaurant in the village and it opened on market day only. The only hotel in the village did not have a restaurant and although I stayed with families on some of my trips, where the food was so wonderful, there were times when I stayed in the Hotel Tonalá and had nowhere to eat. So the market was the best place to go for food. The *liquados* and cakes there were really good and the girls there were always friendly. They still have a knowing smile on their faces whenever they see me! For my mid morning and mid afternoon breaks I always went to their market stall for cake and freshly squeezed juice, or a fresh fruit milkshake.

Pátzcuaro in Michoacán is another place I have left with fond memories of amazing cakes. They are sold on the street of the old square, just outside the small coffee shops. You can sit and eat cake there or buy it to take away. If you

like someone else's cakes outside, they don't mind you bringing theirs in for coffee!

I have included some recipes of cakes that remind me of those early days in Tonalá and Pátzcuaro. Generally in Mexico cakes are much bigger than those you see in the United Kingdom. I have never really understood small cakes, as they never seem to last long. To give you an idea of the scale of things in Mexico, it is not uncommon to find twelve eggs listed under recipe ingredients!

Pastel de queso y nuez
Cheese and nut cake

Ingredients:
180 grams cream cheese
250 grams self-raising flour
150 grams sugar
150 grams crème frâiche
Grated peel and juice of one lemon
5 eggs separated

Decoration:
Apricot jam
25 walnuts

Equipment:
24 cm diameter spring form baking tin

Preparation:
Pre-heat the oven to 180°C, 350°F, Gas Mark 4. Whip the cheese with the sugar until creamy. Add the egg yolks one at a time. Add the flour and crème frâiche alternately, then the lemon peel and juice. Whip the egg whites until they stand in peaks. Fold them carefully into the mixture until all is well mixed. Turn into a greased 24 cm spring form baking tin with removable sides. Bake at 180°C, 350°F, Gas Mark 4 for 15 minutes then turn the temperature down to 150°C, 300°F, Gas Mark 3. Bake for a further 40 minutes until golden and a cake needle inserted in the centre comes out clean. Leave to cool in the tin.

Torta del cielo
Heavenly cake

Sweet and cake recipes based on almonds are very popular in the State of Yucatán in Southern Mexico as almonds are cultivated in the region. *Torta del cielo* is a very large cake: if you want to make a smaller version, or do not have a large enough tin, make it using half the quantities. As this cake contains no wheat flour, it is suitable for those on a gluten-free diet.

Ingredients:
500 grams blanched almonds finely ground (you can buy these ready ground)
500 grams sugar
10 eggs separated
1 tablespoon cornflower
½ teaspoon baking powder
½ teaspoon cream of tartar
½ tablespoon brandy
Icing sugar for dusting

Equipment:
30 cm diameter spring form baking tin (for half the quantity 24 cm)

Preparation:
Pre-heat the oven to 170°C, 325°F, Gas Mark 3. Grease and line the tin with greaseproof paper. Mix together the ground almonds, cornflower and baking powder and set aside.

Beat the egg whites and cream of tartar in a large bowl with an electric mixer, until the egg whites form soft peaks. Add the sugar little by little, beating continuously until the peaks have a gloss. Add the egg yolks one at the time, beating until all the egg yolks are used. Fold in the almonds with a large metal spoon, taking great care not to loose any air, then add the brandy. Turn the mixture into the baking tin and bake for about one hour until golden and a cake needle inserted in the centre comes out clean. Handle carefully: a strong draft or loud noise (such as banging the

oven door) might upset the cake.

Remove from the oven and place the cake, still in the tin, on a wire rack for 5 minutes.. Take great care when removing the cake from the tin or it might collapse in the middle. Leave to cool, then transfer to a large plate and dust with icing sugar.

Pastel de coco y tequila
Coconut and tequila cake

See the chapter: *Agave and Drinks* for this coconut and tequila cake.

Above: spirit of the pineapple paper cut. San Pablito, Puebla.

Notes

Mayahuél, the ancient goddess of the maguey (Agave). Codex Borbónico.

Agave

El maguey - Metl - Agave

'What points a finger at the sky?' taunts an Aztec riddle. The answer: a plant the Aztecs had so many uses for, it was held sacred. Agave was used to make paper, strong rope or cord and thread for garments and footwear; the leaves served as f e n c i n g , firewood and roof coverings; the thorns were used to make tacks and nails; the juice from the plant's central cavity became syrup, vinegar, sugar, and once fermented, 'wine' or *pulque*; the cuticle of the leaf was used to wrap food (ancient cling film) and the root pulp as soap. Today the agave is even used as a washing line!

A man draws *aguamiel* (honey water) from the centre of the agave plant with a gourd. This juice is fermented to make *pulque*.

Pulque

Pulque is the name of a milky white, mildly alcoholic beverage made from the fermented juices of the agave plant. Excavations at the great Pyramid of Cholula, Puebla in 1968, revealed a mural of merry *pulque* drinkers dating to around 1000 AD, though the drink itself is thought to be some 2000 years old. Rich in vitamins and minerals, *pulque* was renowned for its virility, fertility and as an aphrodisiac. So sacred was this agave juice that it was considered an acceptable substitute for blood in certain rituals. The Aztecs called the beverage *octili poliqhui*, which the Spanish later interpreted as *pulque*.

The goddess and incarnation of the maguey plant was Mayahúel. A host of other gods were associated with

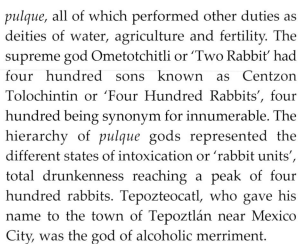

pulque, all of which performed other duties as deities of water, agriculture and fertility. The supreme god Ometotchtli or 'Two Rabbit' had four hundred sons known as Centzon Tolochintin or 'Four Hundred Rabbits', four hundred being synonym for innumerable. The hierarchy of *pulque* gods represented the different states of intoxication or 'rabbit units', total drunkenness reaching a peak of four hundred rabbits. Tepozteocatl, who gave his name to the town of Tepoztlán near Mexico City, was the god of alcoholic merriment.

For the Aztecs, *pulque* had religious and ceremonial significance. It was used as a ritual intoxicant for priests, was served to warriors to celebrate heroic feats in battle, and was offered to sacrificial victims. Rich in basic nutrients, *pulque* was also a medicinal drink that brought strength to the body, and was served to the elderly and nursing mothers. Drunkenness was not tolerated in Aztec society and was a special privilege of the elderly. The general public were only permitted to drink on certain public holidays.

Above: drunkeness was normally frowned upon in Aztec society. An insciption in spanish explains that this seventy year old man may drink freely because he has reached old age, and has children and grandchildren. Codex Mendoza.

Pulque is still produced in Mexico today, particularly in rural areas, where growers believe their plants receive cosmic energy. When the agave reaches maturity, the central *pine* is removed, leaving a cavity. This fills with a sap called *aguamiel* (honey water) when scraped. Siphoning with a long gourd called *acocote* draws off the *aguamiel*. This is held in vats or urns in a sacred fermenting house called *tinacal*.

When the Spanish arrived in Mexico in the sixteenth century, they brought with them the technique of distillation. *Pulque,* with its earthy, vegetal taste, was less popular among the conquistadors than the beers, brandys and wines they were accustomed to. Early attempts to distil *pulque* yielded a harsh, bitter spirit. The breakthrough for the Spanish came when they discovered that cooking the agave pulp resulted in a sweeter juice. Once fermented and distilled, this spirit was known as *mezcal*.

Mezcal and tequila

Mezcal is the name given to all drinks which are obtained from the distilled juices of the agave. The name of the drink depends on where it is produced and the type of agave it comes from. Oaxaca is famous for its *mezcales*, and many bear the name of the village where they are produced. In 1656, the village of Tequila in Jalisco developed a reputation for producing *mezcal* with a superior taste. In 1795, a license was granted to a man named José Cuervo to produce *mezcal* from blue Agave. This spirit came to be known as *tequila* after the area where it is produced. The distinction between *tequila* and *mezcal* is simple. *Tequila* is a *mezcal* derived from one particular plant, the *Agave tequilana Weber blue. Mezcal,* on the other hand, is made from the fermented juices of other agave plants. A useful analogy is *brandy,* a generic name like *mezcal. Cognac* is a superior brandy produced in a specific region, just as *tequila* is a *mezcal* produced in Jalisco. There is also a distinction in the production process. To produce *tequila,* the core of the agave plant, or *piña* (pineapple), is baked in steam ovens or autoclaves, whereas *mezcal* is produced in underground ovens, heated with charcoal, resulting in a rougher, smokier taste.

Below: a scribes text explains that this woman, wife of the man above, left, may drink freely because of her age. Codex Mendoza.

The production of *tequila* is strictly regulated. For a bottle to bear the name *tequila* and receive the *100% Agave* label, the spirit must be at least 51% derived from the Agave tequilana plant, and must be cultivated and distilled in Mexico in the states of Jalisco, Michoacán, Guanajuato, Nayarit or Tamaulipas. Many 'unauthorised' foreign variations of *tequila* now exist bearing similar names, for agave is produced in other parts of the world. The name *tequila* could have various meanings in the indigenous nahuatl language: one is 'place of work' from *téquitl* meaning 'work' and *tlan* meaning 'place'. Another could be 'place of cutting' from the verb *tequi,* ' to cut' and *tlan,* 'place'.

You will never find a worm in a bottle of *tequila*, despite what advertisers will have you believe. However, in a bottle of *mezcal*, you may find the larva of one of two moths that live on the agave plant. The *Hipopta Agavis*, or *gusano rojo* (red worm) is a benign plague, considered a delicacy in Oaxaca, and is used to make salt and *salsas* (sauces). Some maintain that the *gusano* gives the *mezcal* flavour and fragrance. Cynics say that the worm masks the chemical taste of poorly produced *mezcal* and that it is simply an advertising gimmick. There may be a practical explanation; that the worm is 'proof of high-proof'. If the worm remains intact, the percentage of alcohol in the spirit is high enough to preserve the pickled worm. Whatever the reason, you will rarely find a worm in a quality bottle of *mezcal*. Where the worm is found, it can be consumed without harm and doing so has become a ritual of machismo and a rite of passage. Some of the best *mezcales* today are found in Oaxaca, the chief agave employed in its production being the *Agave angustifolia Haw.*

Above: detail from the mural of the *pulque* drinkers, Cholula, Puebla c.1000 AD.

Types of tequila

Blanco - *white or silver*
Colourless *tequila* bottled soon after distillation.
Reposado - *rested*
Tequila rested in wooden barrels (typically oak) for a minimum of 2 months, but not longer than a year.
Añejo - *aged*
The best quality *tequila*, aged in oak barrels for a minimum period of 1 year (there are 400 varieties of oak in Mexico).

How to drink tequila

Most people outside Mexico think there is just one way to drink *tequila*: in short, sharp shots: nothing could be further from the truth. I only ever drink *tequila* this way with European, American or Australian friends. When my Mexican friends drink *tequila* (and they usually have a quality *reposado* or *añejo* bottle at hand), they sip it slowly so that the flavour may be appreciated, like a bottle of fine Malt Whisky.

How you should drink your *tequila* depends on the type of bottle you have and personal preference. White *tequilas* are most often used for mixing and preparing cocktails, though there is some extremely good white *tequila* that is drunk on its own. Popular cocktails are *margaritas,* made with *tequila*, Cointreau and lime juice and *sangrita,* made with *tequila*, orange juice, lemon, *chile* and salt. *Tequila sunrise* is made with orange juice and grenadine.

It is common to accompany *tequila* with lemon and salt. To do so, lick the skin between the thumb and forefinger of your hand and sprinkle with salt. Sip the *tequila* (or drink it all at once), lick the salt, and suck the lime. *Reposado* and *añejo tequilas* are usually taken on their own to conserve the flavour and aroma of the agave. *Tequila* is served in special narrow *tequila* glasses and margaritas in elegant cocktail glasses.

Below: figure from the mural of the *pulque* drinkers, Cholula, Puebla.

Cocktail margarita

Margarita Cocktail

Use fresh limes for a quality margarita cocktail. The proportions are generally 2 parts *tequila*, 1 part Cointreau and 1 part lime juice.

Ingredients:

120 ml white *tequila*
60 ml Cointreau or Triple Sec
60 ml lime juice
I lime
Crushed ice
Salt
(Serves 6 people)

Preparation:

Rub the rim of your cocktail glasses with a segment of the lime. Place the glasses upside down on a plate of salt so that the rims are frosted with salt. Cut thin slices of lime and decorate each glass with a slice. Chill the glasses if you can. Mix the *tequila*, cointreau and lime juice in a jug or cocktail mixer. Serve with ice in the cocktail glasses.

Alternatives: You can also crush the ice and liquid in a blender for a margarita frappé. For a weaker cocktail, mix with grapefruit or other fruit juices.

Right: spirit of the orange paper cut. San Pablito, Puebla.

Agua de jamaica
Hibiscus water drink

Freshly made *aguas* are popular drinks in Mexico and look wonderful on the table.

Ingredients:
100 grams dried Hibiscus flowers
2 ½ litres water
250 grams sugar
Juice of one lime (optional)

Preparation:
Boil the Hibiscus flowers with half a litre of water for 15 minutes. Strain the water into a jug. Add the sugar to the water and dissolve before adding the rest of the water and the lime juice. Serve cold.

Agua de limon
Lime water drink

Ingredients:
100 grams sugar or to taste
8 to 10 limes
1½ litres water

Preparation:
Dissolve the sugar in a little hot water. Pour the water into a jug and add the juice of the limes and the sugar. Stir to mix well. You can also puree the limes whole in a blender with some of the water. Add this pureed mixture to the water and sugar and mix well. As the mixture will be bitter when using the whole lime, you might like to add more sugar and water.

Margarita dessert

This is a wonderfully refreshing dessert, perfect for the summer.

Ingredients:
200 grams caster sugar
200 ml liquid made up of:
      120 ml *tequila*
       80 ml orange juice mixed with the juice of the lime
4 eggs separated
1 lime
1 tablespoon of gelatine
2 tablespoons of cold water for the gelatine

For garnish:
Finely grated rind of lime

Preparation:
Place the two tablespoons of cold water in a pan, sprinkle the gelatine granules over and leave to soak.

Meanwhile whisk the egg whites until they form stiff peaks. Add some of the sugar, continue to whisk and leave aside. Then whisk the egg yolks and the rest of the sugar until creamy and light in colour.

Now go back to the gelatine and dissolve it over a very low heat. Do not allow it to boil. Pour in the *tequila* and juice mixture and mix well. Then add this liquid to the whisked egg yolk and mix well. Chill in the fridge for about 10 minutes or until the egg and *tequila* mixture begins to set. Then gently fold the whisked egg whites into the set yolk mixture, with a metal spoon. Place in a serving dish and keep in the fridge until set. This dessert tastes better chilled.

Pastel de coco y tequila
Coconut and tequila cake

This cake has to be planned well in advance, as the coconut has to be soaked in *tequila* for a week!

Ingredients:
500 grams flour
250 grams sugar
250 grams margarine
4 eggs
100 grams (1 mug) desiccated coarse coconut
200 ml (1 mug) *tequila*
1 teaspoon vanilla essence
½ teaspoon almond essence
3 tablespoons cold water
3 tablespoons cold milk
(both to be added to the egg mixture at the same time as the flour)

Preparation:
Spoon the coconut into a bowl and pour the *tequila* over it. Cover and leave to soak for one week before making the cake.

Equipment: 24 or 26 cm diameter spring form baking tin

A week later...
Pre-heat the oven to 170°C, 325°F, Gas Mark 3. Cream the margarine and sugar. Add the eggs one at the time, whipping continuously. Fold in the coconut/*tequila* mixture, almond and vanilla essence. Gradually add the flour and at the same time pour in the cold water and milk. Spoon the mixture into a greased 24/26cm spring form baking tin. Bake in a pre-heated oven for 30 minutes at 170°C, 325°F, Gas Mark 3 and then increase to 190°C, 375°F, Gas Mark 5. Bake for another 30 minutes until golden and a knife inserted in the centre of the cake comes out clean. This cake keeps very well so can be baked in advance.

Author's Note

I have never been one to make New Year's resolutions. They only make you feel guilty later on when you discover they are impossible to keep up with. Last year I had a wonderful Christmas Eve dinner with family and friends. On Christmas day I took my son Alexander to Heathrow Airport and saw him embark on a long trip to Australia. During the days that followed, I sat in the peace and tranquillity of my world. Looking through my old papers I realised I had started to make notes for this book back in 1996, but the note books had been left on the book shelf, while my life took other turns.

This year I decided I had to do something about it, so I made the resolution to get the book ready starting in the New Year. The bulk of the work had been done, and I knew Anna had much material from her school and university days, as well as from the educational projects and exhibitions we have undertaken over the years. I felt sure that this year I would keep to my resolution.

Anna and I traveled to China in March, a wish I have had all my life. Later in the year The Royal Academy of Arts in London asked for help sourcing products for sale at their shop, for their forthcoming Exhibition, *Aztecs*. At the beginning of July I went to Mexico for ten days, to do work that would normally take a month.

As time for working on the book was getting shorter, Anna and I worked together until the early hours, throughout the summer and early Autumn. We had so much material that I felt sure we could publish a second edition later on, add more recipes and expand on the history and the arts of Mexico.

Shortly afterwards, I learned that I had chronic lymphocytic leukaemia. I am assured that this is mild condition. It may be that I have many years ahead of me, but then again, I may not. I feel that having kept my New Year's resolution has been a twist of fate, one that I shall cherish.

Chonette 2002

Products of American Origin

English Name	Spanish Name	Nahuatl Name	Botanical Name
Agave	Maguey	Metl	Agave spp.
Amaranth	Amaranto, Alegria, Quintonil	Huautli, Huajquilitl, Tzoalli	Amaranthus leucocarpus Amaranthus cruentus
Avocado	Aguacate, Ahuacate	Ahoacatl, Ahoacacuáhuitl	Persea americana
Bean	Frijol, Ejote	Etl, Yetziatli	Phaseolus vulgaris Phaseolus coccineus
Black persimmon, Ebony fruit	Zapote prieto, Zapote negro	Tliltzápotl	Diospyros virginiana Diospyros dignya
Chayote	Chayote	Chayutli, Chayoj	Sechium edule
Chewing gum, zapodilla	Hule, chicle,	Xicotzápotl	Manilkara zapota
Chilli	Chile	Tzilli, Chilli	Capsicum spp.
Cocoa, Chocolate	Cacao, Chocolate	Cacahoaquahuitl, Cacaoacuáhuitl	Theobroma cacao
Cotton	Algodon	Ichcatl	Gossypium spp.
Dahlia	Dalia		Dahlia
Fat Hen / Worseed	Epazote	Epazotl	Chenopodium ambrosoides
Guava	Guayaba	Chalxocotl	Psidium guajava
Jerusalen artichoke			Helianthus tuberosus
Jicama	Jicama	Xicama	Pachyrhizus erosus
Maize	Maiz	Tlaoli, Tlaolli, Centl	Zea mays
Marigold	Pericon, Cempazuchitl	Yianhtli, Zempoaxochitl	Tagetes lucida, Tagetes erecta
Mexican hawthorn	Tejocote	Texoctl	Crataegus mexicana
Mexican oregano	Oregano	Ahuiyac-xihuitl	Lippia graveolens
Nopal cactus/Prickly pear (fruit)	Nopal /Tuna (fruta)	Xoconoxtli Tlatoca-nochtli	Opuntia joconostle Opuntia microdasys
Nopal	Nopal	Nopalli, Nochtli	Opuntia ficus-indica
Pawpaw	Papaya	Papoya	Carica species
Peanut	Cacahuate	Tlalcacáhuatl	Arachis hypogaea
Pineapple	Piña	Mazatli	Ananas comosus
Poinsettia	Flor de Nochebuena	Cuetlaxochitl	Euphobia pulcherrima
Potato	Papa		Solanum tuberosum
Pumpkin, Squash ,Marrow Courgette, Zucchini	Calabaza , Calabacita	Ayutli / Ayojti	Cucurbita spp.
Rubber	Hule	Olicuahuitl	Castilloa elastica
Rubber	Caucho	Cauchú	Hevea brasiliensis
India Rubber tree	Hule	Olcuahitl	Ficus elastica
Sunflower	Girasol	Chimal-acatl	Helianthus annuus
Sweet potato	Camote	Camotli	Ipomoea batatas
Tomatillo	Tomatillo	Tomatl, Miltomatl	Physalis ixocarpa
Vanilla	Vainilla	Tlixcóchitl, Cuomecaxot	Vanilla planifolia
Wild sage	Chia	Chia	Salvia hispanica

Suppliers

of Mexican Products and Services

b.right.on food co
Tel.01273 705606
Web site: *www.hanovernet.co.uk/brightchili.htm*

Cool Chile Company (chiles)
PO Box 5702
London, W11 2 GS
Tel. 0870 9021145, Fax 0870 056 2288
Email: *dodie@coolchile.demon.co.uk*
Web site: *www.coolchile.co.uk*

El Azteca
2 The Mews,
Elephant & Castle Shopping Centre
London, SE1 6TE
Tel/Fax: 020 7708 4141
E-mail: *elaztecalondon@hotmail.com*
Web site: *www.elaztecafood.co.uk*

Future Foods (seed suppliers)
Luckleigh Cottage, Hockworthy
Wellington Somerset, TA21 0NN
Tel. 01398 361347, Fax: 01398 361541
Web site: *www.futurefoods.com*

Lupe Pintos Deli
Edinburgh:
24 Leven Street, EH3 9LJ
Tel. 0131 228 6241
Glasgow:
313 Great Western Road
Tel. 0141 334 5444
E-mail: *lupep@gxn.co.uk*
Web site: *www.lupepintos.com*

Mexicolore (piñatas and educational)
28 Warriner Gardens
London, SW11 4EB
Tel. 0207 622 9577, Fax: 0207 498 3643
Web site: *www.mexicolore.co.uk*

Peppers by Post
Sea Spring Farm
West Bexington
Dorchester, Dorset, DT2 9DD
Tel. 01308 897892, Fax: 01308 897735
Fresh chillies poblanos and tomatillos in season (July to Nov.)

Quetzal (shop, restaurant and education department)
61 New Road
Chippenham, Wiltshire, SN15 1ES
Tel. 01249 652496
Web site: *www.quetzal-uk.com*
E-mail: *info@quetzal-uk.com*

Seasoned Pioneers Ltd.
101 Summers Road,
Brunswick Business Park,
Liverpool, L3 4BJ
Tel/Fax: 0151 709 9330, Free phone: 0800 0682348
E-mail: *info@seasonedpioneers.co.uk*
Web site: *www.seasonedpioneers.co.uk*

The Spice Shop
1 Blenheim Crescent
London, W11 2EE
Tel. 020 7 221 4448, Fax: 020 7229 1591
Web site: *www.thespiceshop.co.uk*

Good Web site
Web site: *www.chillisgalore.co.uk*

Visit the Eden project in Cornwall to explore plants of
Mexican origin in their natural environment
www.edenproject.com

Bibliography

Bagust, Harold. *The Gardener's Dictionary of Horticulture Terms*. London: Cassell Publishers, 1996.

Bayless, Rick and Bayless, Deam Groen. *Authentic Mexican Regional Cooking from the Heart of Mexico*. New York: William Morrow & Company, 1987.

Bianchini, F. and Corbeta, F. *The Fruits of the Earth*. London: Bloombury Books, 1975.

Boatfield, Graham. *Farm Crops*. London: Farming Press, 1983.

Brickell, Christopher. ed. *The Royal Horticultural Society Encyclopedia of Gardening*. London: Dorling Kindersley, 1998.

Caplan, Basil. ed. *The Complete Manual of Organic Gardening*. London: Headlline Book Publishing, 1994.

Carrillo, Ana María. *La Cocina del Tomate Frijol y Calabaza. La Cocina Mexicana A Través de los Siglos*. Mexico City: Editorial Clío, 1998.

Catelló Yturbide, T. and Piña Luján, I. *Presencia de la comida Prehispanica*. Mexico City: Fondo de Cultura Banamex, 1987.

Coe, D. Sophie and Coe, D. Michael. *The True History of Chocolate*. London: Thames and Hudson, 1996.

Cordell, Linda S. and Foster, Nelson ed. *Chilies to Chocolate: Food the Americas Gave to the World*. Arizona: The University of Arizona Press, 1992.

Cruces Carvajal, Ramon. *Lo Que Mexico Aporto al Mundo*. Mexico City: Panorama Editorial, 1987.

Díaz del Castillo, Bernal. Translated by Cohen, J.M. *The Conquest of New Spain*. London: Penguin Books, 1987.

Enciso, Jorge. *The Design Motifs of Ancient Mexico*. New York: Dover Publications, 1959.

Espejel, Carlos. *Las Artesanias Tradicionales en Mexico*. Mexico City: Editorial Blume, 1972.

Esquivel, Laura. *Como Agua para Chocolate*. Barcelona: Salvat Editores, 1994.

Fernandez, Adela. *La tradicional comida Mexicana y sus mejores recetas*. Mexico City: Panorama Editorial, 1988.

Guía Mexico Desconocido Numero 135: *Chiles* pp. 10-15. Mexico City: Editorial Jilguero, 1988.

Frances, F. Berdan and Patricia, Rieff Anawalt. *The Essential Codex Mendoza*. California: University of California Press, 1997.

Frost, Louise and Griffiths, Alistair. *Plants of Eden*. Penzance: Alison Hodge, 2001.

Garcia Acosta, Virginia. *Los Senores del Maiz*. Mexico city: Pangea Editores, 1991.

Garcia Rivas, Heriberto. C*ocina Prehispanica Mexicana*. Mexico City: Panorama Editorial, 1991.

Geddes, Bruce. *World Food: Mexico*. Victoria: Lonely Planet Publications, 2000.

Guía Mexico Desconocido/Antojitos Numero 44. Mexico City: Editorial Mexico Desconocido, 1998.

Guía Mexico Desconocido Numero 135: *Chiles* pp. 10-15. Mexico City: Editorial Jilguero, 1988.

Hansen, Barbara. *Mexican Cookery*. Tucson, USA: H.P. Books, 1980.

Horcasitas, Fernando. *The Aztecs Then and Now.* Mexico City: Editorial Minutiae Mexicana, 1988.

Kennedy, Diana. *The Cuisines of Mexico.* New York: Harpers and Row, 1972.

Lewington, Anna. *Plants for people.* London: Natural History Museum Publications, 1990.

Lomeli, Arturo. *El Arte de Cocinar con Chiles.* Mexico City: Editorial Contenido, 1986.

Long, Solis Janet and Alvarez Aranzazu Camarena, Manuel. *El Placer del Chile.* Mexico City: Editorial Clío, 1998.

Martínez Maximino. *Catálogo de nombres vulgares y científicos de plantas mexicanas.* Mexico City: Fondo de Cultura Económica, 1979.

Martinez, Zarela. *Food From My Heart: Cuisines of Mexico Remembered and Reimagined.* New York: Macmillan Publishing, 1992.

Meyer, Karl E. *Teotihuacan.* London: The Reader's Digest Association with Newsweek, New York, 1973.

Museo Nacional de Culturas Populares, *El Maiz.* Mexico City: Garcia Valades Editores, September 1987.

Museo Nacional de Culturas Populares. *El Universo del Amate.* Mexico City: Garcia Valades Editores, 1987.

Novo, Salvador. *Cocina Mexicana o Historia Grastronomica de la Ciudad de Mexico.* Mexico City: Editorial Porrua, 1973.

Palazuelos, Susanna and Tausend, Marilyn. *Mexico The Beautiful Cook Book.* London: Merehurst Limited, 1993.

Pasztory, Esther *Pre-Columbian Art.* London: The Orion Publishing Group, 1998.

Phillips, Roger and Rix, Martyn. *Vegetables*. London: Macmillan Publishers, 1995.

Reader's Digest Encyclopaedia of Garden Plants and Flowers. 1972 edition.

Rivera, Maria. *Un buen aguacero sale en 1,500 pesos*. [WWW] http://www.jornada.unam.mx (25th May 2002)

Ross, Kurt. *Codex Mendoza, Aztec Manuscript*. Fribourg: Productions Liber, 1978.

Sackmann, Wolfgang et al. *Wer den Ton Beseelt...cerámica mexicana*. Hildesheim: El Puente, 1986.

Sandstrom, Alan R. and Pamela, Effrein. *Traditional Papermaking and Paper Cult Figures of Mexico*. London: Norman and London, 1986.

Santiago Cruz, Francisco. *La Conquista Florida*. Mexico City: Editorial Jus, 1973.

Smith E. Michael. *The Aztecs*. Oxford: Blackwell Publishers, 1996.

Solis, Felipe. *La Cultura del Maiz*. Mexico City: Editorial Clío, 1998.

Soustelle, Jacques. Translated by O'Brian, Patrick. *Daily Life of the Aztecs*. London: Pelican Books, 1964.

Stuart, Gene S. *The Mighty Aztecs*. Washington: National Geographic Society, 1981.

Taibo, Ignacio. *Brevario del Mole Poblano*. Mexico City: Editorial Terra Nova, 1981.

The Royal Horticulture Society Gardener's Encyclopaedia of Plants and Flowers. Dorling Kindersley Ltd. London (1989).

Vaughan, John Griffith. *The New Oxford book of food plants: a guide to the fruit, vegetables, herbs and spices of the world*. London: Oxford University Press, 1999.

Index of Recipes

Credits

References

Introduction pp18-19: excerpt from Fernandez, Adela. *La tradicional comida Mexicana y sus mejores recetas.* Mexico City: Panorama Editorial, 1988

The Market pp25, 33, Cocoa 164-165: excerpts from Diaz del Castillo, Bernal. Translation by Cohen, J.M. *The Conquest of New Spain.* London: Penguin Books, 1987.

Picture Credits

Line Drawings

Illustrations are identified by their page numbers in bold.

Alberto Beltran: from Horcasitas, Fernanando. *The Aztecs Then and Now.* Mexico City: Editorial Minutuae Mexicana, 1988: **28, 32 above, 35**

Jose Narro: from Cruces, Carvajal, Ramon. *Lo Que Mexico Aporto al Mundo.* Mexico City: Panorama Editorial, 1987: **24**

Pre-Hispanic flat stamp design motifs: *Jorge Enciso:* from *The Design Motifs of Ancient Mexico.* New York: Dover Publications, 1959

All other illustrations are by the author © Anna Xochitl Taylor

Cover photographs

© Anna Xochitl Taylor

The authors are grateful to publishers for granting permission to reproduce images and excepts in this book. Every effort has been made to trace copyright holders. Any omissions are unintentional and we would be pleased to add acknowledgements in future editions.

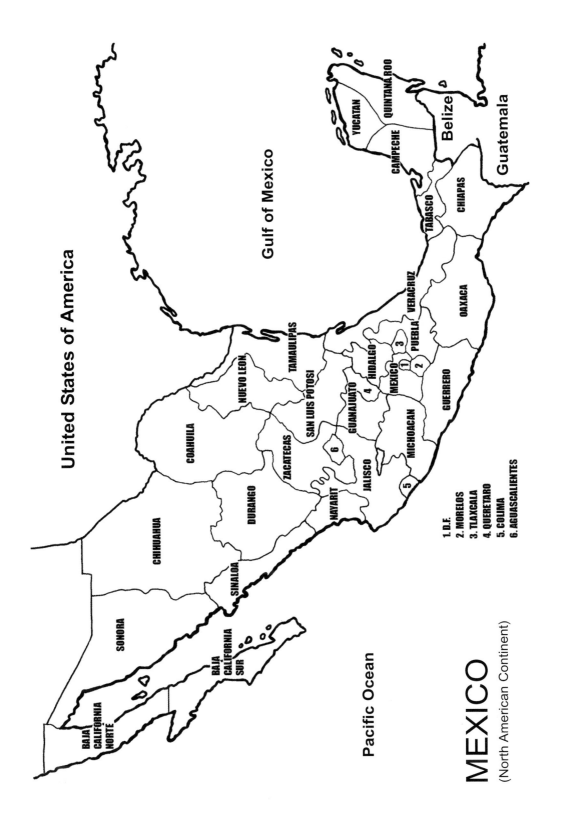

MEXICO
(North American Continent)

1. D.F.
2. MORELOS
3. TLAXCALA
4. QUERETARO
5. COLIMA
6. AGUASCALIENTES

219

Notes